POLICY RESEARCH PROJECT PARTICIPANTS

Joanne Bogart, B.A. (History/American Studies), Austin College
Christopher Bradley, B.A. (Political Science), Washington
    and Lee University
John C. Dougherty, B.A. (General Studies), Antioch
    University West
Rebecca Lancaster, B.S. (Public Administration), University
    of Arkansas
Peter McCanna, A.B. (English), University of Michigan at
    Ann Arbor
Melanie Morgan, B.A. (Communication Arts and Sciences),
    Michigan State University
Beth Ryshavy, B.A. (Government), St. Benedict College
Laura Scott, B.A. (Political Science), University of Florida
Cathy Stahl, B.A. (Government), University of Texas at Austin
Barbara Steakley, B.A. (Political Science), University
    of Houston
Min Bong You, B.A. (Public Administration), Sung Kyun Kwan
    University, Seoul, Korea
John Zapata, B.A. (Urban Science and Planning), University
    of California at San Diego

Project Director

W. Norton Grubb, Associate Professor, Lyndon B. Johnson
    School of Public Affairs

Table of Contents

FOREWORD

The Lyndon B. Johnson School of Public Affairs has established interdisciplinary research on policy problems as the core of its educational program. A major part of this program is the nine-month policy research project, in the course of which one or two faculty members from different disciplines direct the research of ten to twenty graduate students of diverse backgrounds on a policy issue of concern to a government agency. This "client orientation" brings the students face to face with administrators, legislators, and other officials active in the policy process and demonstrates that research in a policy environment demands special talents. It also illuminates the occasional difficulties of relating research findings to the world of political realities.

This report on the initial effects of House Bill 72 is the result of a policy research project conducted in 1984-85 under grants from Texans for Quality Education and from the Lyndon B. Johnson Foundation. House Bill 72 was a comprehensive bill passed during a special legislative session in the summer of 1984, with provisions designed both to make the financing of education more equitable and to improve the effectiveness of public schooling. Relying on information from extensive interviews as well as district finances, this monograph examines the effects of the legislation on financing patterns, on practices affecting both teachers and students, on programs for special groups (including compensatory education, bilingual education, special education for handicapped children, and vocational education), and on new preschool programs. These findings are the basis for a series of recommendations addressed to policymakers, educators, and citizens concerned about public education.

The curriculum of the LBJ School is intended not only to develop effective public servants but also to produce research that will enlighten and inform those already engaged in the policy process. The project that resulted in this report has helped to accomplish the first task; it is our hope and expectation that the report itself will contribute to the second.

Finally, it should be noted that neither the LBJ School nor the University of Texas at Austin necessarily endorses the views or findings of this study.

Max Sherman
Dean

ACKNOWLEDGMENTS

This study of the implementation of the 1984 Texas Education Reform Bill, House Bill 72, was made possible by grants from Texans for Quality Education and from the Lyndon B. Johnson Foundation. The findings and interpretations in this report are solely those of the authors, however, and Texans for Quality Education and the LBJ Foundation are not responsible for any errors of fact or interpretation.

Our greatest debt is to the teachers and administrators we interviewed in school districts throughout the state. We would especially like to thank the following individuals for coordinating and arranging interviews in their respective districts: Wayne Blevins (superintendent, Abilene ISD); Arnold Oates (superintendent, Brazosport ISD); Raul Bestiero (superintendent, Brownsville ISD); Julian Shaddix (superintendent, Clint ISD); K. Allen Johnson (assistant superintendent, El Paso ISD); Patricia Shell (assistant superintendent, Houston ISD); Maurice Rawlings (assistant superintendent, Hurst-Euless-Bedford ISD); Preston Stephens (superintendent, La Vernia ISD); Bill Walker (assistant superintendent, Ector County ISD); Lee Meyer (superintendent, Pasadena ISD); Ron Knight (finance officer, Plano ISD); Don Taylor (superintendent, Roosevelt ISD); William C. Grussendorf (superintendent, San Saba ISD); Bill Sybert (superintendent, Socorro ISD); Rip Lasater (superintendent, Sundown ISD); Bill Borgers (superintendent, Taylor ISD); Jack Davidson (superintendent, Tyler ISD); and Irma Gonzales (assistant superintendent, Weslaco ISD).

We thank Cindy Holdway of the Texas Association of School Boards and Johnny Veselka of the Texas Association of School Administrators for the data used in this study. Maureen Scheevel, Grace Dunn, and Tom Mee of the Texas Education Agency were helpful in providing computer tapes of TEA data. We also thank David Thompson of the Texas Association of School Boards for his continuing interest in the project and Craig Foster of the Equity Center for his advice.

This report would not have been completed without the assistance which members of various education groups, the state legislature, and the Texas Education Agency provided. We extend our thanks to all these individuals and hope that this report to which they have contributed will help interpret the effects of the Texas Education Reform Bill and clarify the educational issues that remain before the people of Texas.

Several individuals made helpful comments on initial drafts, and they have helped us avoid errors of fact and interpretation; for this we want to thank Dr. Timy Baranoff, Oscar Cardenas, Pat Longoria, Jose Cardenas, Craig Foster, Cindy Holdway, Johnny Veselka, John Cole, Madeleine McCulley, Maurice Rawlings, and Gary Wood.

INTRODUCTION
THE CLIMATE OF REFORM IN TEXAS

In the summer of 1984, the Texas legislature enacted a massive reform of the state's system of elementary and secondary education. The passage of House Bill 72 resulted from an environment of reform that has existed for several years. Education has been a topic of debate among educators, parents, the business community, social reformers, and politicians around the nation and within Texas. However, the participants in this debate have had major disagreements about the proper direction for educational reforms. Robert M. Hutchins once asserted that "if the purpose of education is the improvement of men, then any system of education that is without values is a contradiction in terms."[1] In determining what to teach, when to teach, and which methods to employ, society makes difficult choices about its values. Since reaching a consensus on values has been especially difficult in our pluralistic society, the history of educational reform in the United States has been quite active.

In a broad sense, reform efforts have emphasized two potentially conflicting values--equity and excellence. In the past thirty years, reforms have shifted in emphasis between the two, with reforms of the 1950s stressing excellence, those of the 1960s and 1970s stressing equity, and those of the 1980s returning to themes of excellence. While excellence and equity are not always in conflict, problems can arise because equity is sometimes interpreted as narrowing the gap in educational achievement, perhaps by holding back those at the top. Conversely, movements for excellence in education have often stressed the education of high-achieving students, with less concern for others. However, House Bill 72 is aimed simultaneously at the enhancement of both equity and excellence or effectiveness in the Texas public schools.

EQUITY IN EDUCATION: THE ISSUES OF ACCESS AND FINANCE

Equity has been a concern of educators since the establishment of public schools in the United States. The equity issue, often guided by the principles of equal opportunity and equal access to schooling, has been most prominent in cases of discrimination on the basis of racial, ethnic, and socioeconomic background. Following the 1954 Supreme Court decision in Brown v. Board of Education, many reforms were concerned with establishing equality of opportunity for children of all races. Steps in this direction included the Civil Rights Act of 1964 and the Elementary and Secondary Education Act of 1965, which provided federal funds for compensatory education designed to provide better schooling for low-income or "disadvantaged" children (including many minority children). The logic of funding compensatory education was then extended to other groups--especially to handicapped children with the passage of Public Law 94-142 in 1974, and to children of limited English proficiency (LEP) with the Bilingual Education Act of 1973.

In the development of compensatory education, bilingual education, and special education, the issue of equity has been entangled with the issue of financing. It is generally assumed that the quality of education is linked to the availability of resources and that, even where overt discrimination is eliminated, inequality of opportunity may still persist because of differences in financing. For example, the Civil Rights Commission report of 1967, Racial Isolation in the Public Schools, asserted that equality of resources is necessary to achieve equal opportunity in education.[2] As a result, reformers have often promoted equal opportunity by attempting to distribute resources more equitably. This logic has in turn been used to attack the differences in expenditures among school districts that result from differences in wealth or property value.

Although attempts to narrow expenditure differences among school districts have a long history,[3] recent reforms have been spurred by various court rulings. One of the first and most important cases was the 1971 decision by the California Supreme Court in Serrano v. Priest. Schools in California--like schools in Texas--received state funding through a foundation plan in which districts would receive money from the state to bring districts up to a minimum level of spending--the so-called foundation. However, the foundation plan allowed districts to use local funds to supplement state aid, and the variation in property wealth among districts allowed wealthy districts to spend huge sums per pupil while poor districts could provide little more than the state-funded minimum. The Serrano case declared this financing system unconstitutional according to the California constitution, on the grounds that it violated guarantees of equal protection. The Serrano decision had a very important national impact, as James W. Guthrie summarized, because:

> . . . it displayed that the equal protection argument could be made on state constitutional grounds, even if the federal argument was eroded. Second, Serrano made it clear that the principle of fiscal neutrality could be fashioned in a manner acceptable to courts in calculating a judicially manageable remedy. Serrano also reinforced the view that legislatures would respond responsibly to judicial school finance mandates.[4]

Robinson v. Cahill, a case decided in May 1973 by the New Jersey Supreme Court, also indicated that reform could be accomplished through court action at the state level, and these two cases were followed by a plethora of cases in other states.[5]

However, in a Texas case reformers failed to win support from the federal courts, with national ramifications. The 1971 Rodriguez case was like many of the others, although the case was brought in federal rather than state court. The development of the Texas public education system from the first years of the state's existence followed a pattern of sporadic increases in state involvement, although local control over the public schools remained an important principle. After the turn of the century, resistance to state funding began to diminish, and concern with the equalization of educational resources increased. In 1915, the legislature appropriated special equalization aid to encourage local tax efforts in rural school districts. The state's role then shifted from encouraging local tax effort to providing state funding for rural school districts. One of the most important pieces of reform was the Gilmer-Aikin Act of 1949, which established the minimum foundation plan (MFP) for state aid to public education. The foundation plan has been the basic allocation method for state aid ever since, although it has seen numerous modifications. The goal of the Gilmer-Aikin plan was that "each student should be given an equal minimum educational opportunity financed by equalized local tax effort and supplemented by state aid sufficient to compensate for the variations in local taxpaying ability."[6] However, the foundation plan permitted a high degree of local control, as districts were allowed to spend more than the minimum plan if they chose to provide more local funds for education.

As in California, it became apparent that the minimum foundation plan allowed substantial differences in spending within Texas. In 1971, a U.S. district court ruled the Texas education finance system unconstitutional in Rodriguez v. San Antonio. This ruling was then reversed by the U.S. Supreme Court in 1973. Although the Rodriguez case was similar to Serrano, it was argued on the grounds of equal protection provisions in the U.S. Constitution rather than those of the state constitution. The U.S. Supreme Court's decision stated that, although Texas's system of educational finance was "chaotic and unjust," it did not violate the federal constitution, for three reasons. First, the Court decided that education was not a "fundamental interest" because it was not mentioned in the federal constitution and therefore did not warrant Court intervention. The Court also noted that the plaintiffs--residents of a low-wealth school district--were not uniformly poor or of a particular racial group and could not prove that a "legally suspect classification" was employed by the State of Texas; because the Texas school finance mechanism was in some sense rational, it was acceptable to the Court. Finally, the Court questioned the connection between funding levels and the quality of education. The result of Rodriguez was that the battle for equity in school finance has been waged on a state-by-state basis, rather than relying on a federal ruling.

Despite being decided against the plaintiffs, the Rodriguez case has had a continuing influence on Texas public education. In the wake of the decision, several studies were performed to recommend changes in school finance, and the Office of Educational Research and Planning within the Texas Education Agency (TEA) was created to correct inequalities that had come to light in the recent litigation.[7] House Bill 1126, passed in 1975, attempted to equalize resources by increasing equalization aid to property-poor districts. Since House Bill 1126 was not judged particularly successful in addressing problems of equalization, Senate Bill 1 was enacted in 1977 to revise equalization aid further. S.B. 1 added $1 billion to the foundation school program, revised local fund assignments, and provided funds for vocational education and special education programs. In 1979, the legislature passed S.B. 350, an attempt to equalize district resources further; S.B. 350 expanded the foundation school program once again, readjusted the local fund assignment, established a floor for aid to small districts, added a fast growth adjustment and a minimum aid adjustment, and provided more support services to small districts. The concern with equity in funding embodied, however imperfectly, in these pieces of legislation set the stage for many of the provisions of House Bill 72.

THE EFFECTIVENESS OF EDUCATION AND THE "EXCELLENCE MOVEMENT"

House Bill 72 was not limited in its scope to educational equity; the issue of quality of education was also of considerable importance to this reform. Reformers like to view excellence and equity as complementary goals, and supporters of reforms aimed at increasing educational quality have often formed coalitions with proponents of equity in order to pass legislation.[8] H.B. 72 is, in many respects, an example of legislation that is the work of such a coalition. But while these two goals should not be in conflict, they are sometimes antagonistic. As Allan Odden summarized the problem:

serious tensions exist between equity and educational excellence. . . . . they arise only when links between excellence and equity are overlooked. School finance reforms have their roots in attempts to improve the quality of education for students in economically deprived school districts. By the same token, the effective schools movement has its roots in attempts to improve the academic performance of poor and minority students. Meanwhile, most of the recent national reports on education have recommended that equity and excellence be pursued simultaneously through measures that benefit all kinds of students.[9]

In practice, reforms concerned with equity have often found themselves to be at cross-purposes with reformers concerned about quality or excellence.

The excellence movement has taken many forms. In many cases, calls for educational reform have linked the success or failure of the public schools to the performance of the economy and the preservation of national security. Education reforms resulting from the Sputnik scare during the 1950s and 1960s, and the reform movements of the 1980s share a fear that public education lacks rigor (especially in the areas of math and science) and makes too few demands on students. Many of these reforms have taken a "back-to-basics" approach. This contrasts with reform movements of the 1970s, which stressed the lack of humaneness and relevance of the public school curriculum and proposed greater flexibility and variety as solutions.[10]

The most recent movement for excellence in education is exemplified by the 1983 report of the National Commission on Excellence in Education, A Nation at Risk: The Imperative for Educational Reform. This report began with the statement, "Our nation is at risk. Our once unchallenged preeminence in commerce, industry, science, and technological innovation is being overtaken by competitors throughout the world," attributing chis to "an act of unthinking, unilateral education disarmament." It then cited familiar evidence about the decline of test scores, the high level of functional illiteracy, and the decline of "higher order intellectual skills." The report made several recommendations aimed primarily at improving teaching quality: raising admission standards at teacher training institutions, raising teachers' salaries, adopting eleven-month contracts for teachers, using career ladders to reward teacher excellence, employing noncertified personnel to cover shortages in fields like math and science, providing loans and grants for qualified students who wish to enter teacher training programs, and introducing the position of "master teachers," who would be involved in designing teacher preparation programs. The report also recommended partnerships between the business community and the public education system and more power for school principals. Many other reports were published in 1983 and 1984, different in their evidence and emphases, but all of them stressed the need to reverse the declining quality of elementary and secondary education.

In Texas, the excellence movement first achieved legislative success with the passage of House Bill 246 by the 66th Texas Legislature in 1981. The purpose of the bill was to improve and standardize the curriculum taught in the state's public schools by establishing twelve basic subject areas judged to be necessary to a sound education. House Bill 246 also addressed the issues of discipline, attendance, and standards for academic promotion. (Because there has been considerable confusion between H.B. 72 and H.B. 246, the curriculum changes of H.B. 246 are analyzed in chapter 9 of this report.) Like the issue of equity, then, the problem of educational quality had generated considerable concern in Texas well before the movement that culminated in House Bill 72.

THE PASSAGE OF HOUSE BILL 72

The Texas legislature was prodded into taking the actions that led to House Bill 72 by a number of different developments. The issues of the Rodriguez case returned to prominence with a similar lawsuit filed in state court on May 23, 1984, by the Mexican American Legal Defense and Educational Fund (MALDEF). The suit, Edgewood v. Bynum, included as plaintiffs the Edgewood Independent School District near San Antonio and a number of other low-wealth districts, as well as students from these districts. The lawsuit claimed that the education system was in violation of the Texas constitution because children in poor school districts were not provided with educational programs "substantially equal to those available to any similar student" in wealthier districts. MALDEF also argued that, because there are concentrations of low-income and Mexican American students in property-poor school districts, the state is practicing discrimination on the basis of wealth and national origin in its education policy, in violation of the equal protection clause of the Texas constitution.[11]

Since the Edgewood v. Bynum case was filed only in May 1984, it would normally have taken several years for a final verdict in the case. Nonetheless, the mere threat of an adverse ruling seems to have been enough to prod the legislature into once again considering fiscal measures to reduce disparities among rich and poor districts. Evidently, the legislature hoped that the equalization measures in House Bill 72, analyzed at greater length in chapter 1, would be sufficient to make any lawsuit moot.

While A Nation at Risk provided a national focus for those concerned with improving educational quality, the work of the Select Committee on Public

Education (SCOPE) was the catalyst necessary for the passage of House Bill 72. Although the recommendations of SCOPE were consistent with those of the nationwide movement for excellence, its genesis and deliberations were more idiosyncratic. Governor Mark White, elected in 1982 with the support of teachers, had pledged to legislate an increase in state aid for teacher salaries. But the 1983 legislature, faced with declining revenues, was unable to pass such an increase without a much-dreaded tax increase. Instead, the legislature authorized SCOPE to study the finance system of the public schools in Texas and to make recommendations for its improvement, recommendations to be considered in 1984 at a special session of the legislature. The structure of SCOPE indicated a firm commitment to reform by influential members of the legislature and the governor's office, and the committee itself included some of the most powerful people in Texas in the area of education policy: Governor Mark White, Lieutenant Governor Bill Hobby, House Speaker Gib Lewis, and other political leaders.[12] The committee was chaired by H. Ross Perot, well-known computer entrepreneur.

In the course of discussing teacher salaries, SCOPE also considered the issue of teacher quality, because of the belief of H. Ross Perot and others that some improvement in teaching was necessary to justify additional state spending. With its purview including almost all aspects of education, SCOPE then considered a variety of measures related to student discipline and standards, the reform of specific programs like vocational education, and innovations like prekindergarten programs and technology education. The final SCOPE report therefore included a large number of recommendations of A Nation at Risk and the national movement for excellence--recommendations that went far beyond the subject of teacher salaries.[13]

Many, although not all, of the SCOPE recommendations were incorporated into House Bill 72, developed and passed by the Texas legislature during a special legislative session that lasted a scant month, from June 4 to July 3, 1984. The process of bargaining and compromise over specific provisions of House Bill 72 was, by all accounts, complex and hurried; in the process, many SCOPE recommendations were abandoned, and new proposals were included.[14] The bill that emerged therefore represents the confluence of many pressures--among them the demands to equalize funding, the movement to improve the quality of teaching, pledges to increase teacher salaries, and the resistance of groups threatened by reform.

House Bill 72 was in many ways a highly centralized or "top-down" reform, directed by the state's political leadership and a few influential individuals like H. Ross Perot. In contrast to reforms in other states, which have involved the educational community and interested citizens in order to build a consensus on reform,[15] the changes in Texas took place with relatively little consultation with local educators and almost no participation by parents and other interested citizens. In fact, the content of the bill itself was generally not known by educators until its final passage, partly because of the haste with which it was put together. The long-run effects of this top-down approach to reform are not clear, especially since most educators appear to have been diligent in responding to the changes in House Bill 72. Nevertheless, it remains important to recognize the particular circumstances surrounding the development of House Bill 72.

THE PLAN OF THIS REPORT

In this report we examine the effects of House Bill 72 during its first year of operation. Because it was such a complex bill, we cannot pretend to have covered all its effects. Instead, we have concentrated on changes in financing; on the reforms intended to improve the quality of teaching and to clarify the responsibilities of students; on the changes in programs for special populations, including compensatory education, bilingual education, special education for handicapped students, and vocational education; and on several innovations, especially in preschool programs.

The first chapter examines the financial measures in House Bill 72, intended to equalize spending among districts by increasing state funds to poor districts while reducing aid to wealthy districts. After describing the various financing components, we describe the initial effects of House Bill 72 on teacher salaries, operating expenditures, the career ladder intended to reward especially able teachers, the requirements for districts to reduce class size, and--most important of all--disparities in spending among rich and poor districts. Our analysis of these initial effects is based on data collected by the Texas Association of School Boards (TASB) and the Texas Association of School Administrators (TASA) and on data available from the Texas Education Agency.

Chapter 2 examines the various reforms aimed at improving the quality of teaching. House Bill 72 attempts to help school districts attract and retain outstanding teachers through increases in teachers' salaries, the establishment of a career ladder, the requirement of a competency test for teachers, and a loan program to attract more people to teaching. Several of these provisions--especially the career ladder and the competency test--have been extremely controversial, suggesting that the good intentions of House Bill 72 might be undermined by the resentment of teachers.

Our third chapter focuses on the measures in House Bill 72 that affect students. House Bill 72 attempts to motivate student achievement in various ways, including a provision that a student must have an average grade of 70 or above to be promoted, an exit exam required for graduation, tutorials for students having difficulty in their subject, and restrictions on absences and extracurricular activities. Many of these have proved to be quite controversial among parents and students and raise the question of how effective state legislation can be in improving practices at the local level.

The next four chapters deal with the effects of House Bill 72 on programs which seek to provide special educational services for students who need them. In the case of compensatory education for disadvantaged students (examined in chapter 4), state funding has been greatly increased, but problems have arisen because of conflicts with federal funding mechanisms. Bilingual education, discussed in chapter 5, faces problems because of a continuing debate over the nature of bilingual education and severe shortages of qualified bilingual teachers. Chapter 6, on special education, focuses on the changes in the state funding mechanism and potential conflicts with federal law. Chapter 7 examines changes in the funding of vocational education and the provisions in House Bill 72 which attempt to make this program more accountable and effective.

In addition to reforming existing programs, House Bill 72 established several new programs. Some, like technology education and community service centers, are merely encouraged, but two--a prekindergarten program for four-year-olds who are disadvantaged or have limited English proficiency and a summer bilingual program for children of limited English proficiency who will be entering kindergarten or first grade--are required. Chapter 8 examines the structure of these two novel programs, both of which extend Texas schools into preschool education.

In the implementation of House Bill 72, a great deal of confusion has arisen because of the simultaneous implementation of another bill--House Bill 246, passed in 1981 and requiring complex changes in curriculum and graduation requirements. Because several provisions of House Bill 72 and House Bill 246 are similar, and because the two bills went into effect at the same time, educators and parents have often blamed House Bill 72 for problems caused by House Bill 246. Therefore, chapter 9 examines the provisions of House Bill 246, in order to clarify the confusion over the two pieces of legislation.

In examining the effects of House Bill 72, we have relied primarily on interviews conducted in 19 districts throughout Texas.[16] Although these districts cannot possibly be considered a random sample of the 1,068 districts in Texas, they were carefully chosen to represent all areas of the state, to include both large urban districts (such as Houston, Fort Worth, and El Paso) as well as small rural districts (such as Sundown and La Vernia). They include several wealthy districts as well as some that are quite poor, and districts with high proportions of minority students (including two in the Valley) as well as districts with few minority students. Table A lists the districts we visited along with some of their characteristics, and figure 1 indicates where they are located.

Interviews in these districts were conducted in January and February of 1985, halfway through the first school year under House Bill 72; follow-up phone calls were made throughout the spring of 1985. In every district we interviewed the superintendent and administrators in charge of finance, personnel, curriculum, and special programs. In addition, we interviewed one or two principals and several representatives of teacher organizations in every district. In this way we hoped to get several different viewpoints on the effects of House Bill 72.

If our sample of districts is biased in any way, we may have examined districts where administrators and teachers are especially motivated,

Table A
Characteristics of Districts Interviewed

	1983-84 Average Daily Attendance	1983-84 Property Value per Pupil	1983-84 Expenditure per Pupil
Alvarado	1,476	$ 90,122	$2,389
Brazosport	10,323	378,939	3,336
Brownsville	28,965	52,585	2,331
Clint	1,160	140,768	2,936
Ector County	22,770	307,154	3,440
El Paso	53,734	113,031	2,681
Fort Worth	57,030	231,315	3,095
Houston	171,444	384,023	3,224
Hurst-Euless-Bedford	15,502	208,901	2,786
La Vernia	753	112,693	2,209
Pasadena	32,073	187,755	2,813
Plano	23,828	233,928	3,760
Roosevelt	1,120	105,812	2,317
San Saba	773	127,510	2,529
Socorro	6,137	58,877	2,650
Sundown	442	2,987,269	7,964
Taylor	2,080	127,561	3,314
Weslaco	8,851	54,300	2,655
Statewide Average	29,754	$233,984	$3,299

Figure 1
Location of Districts Interviewed

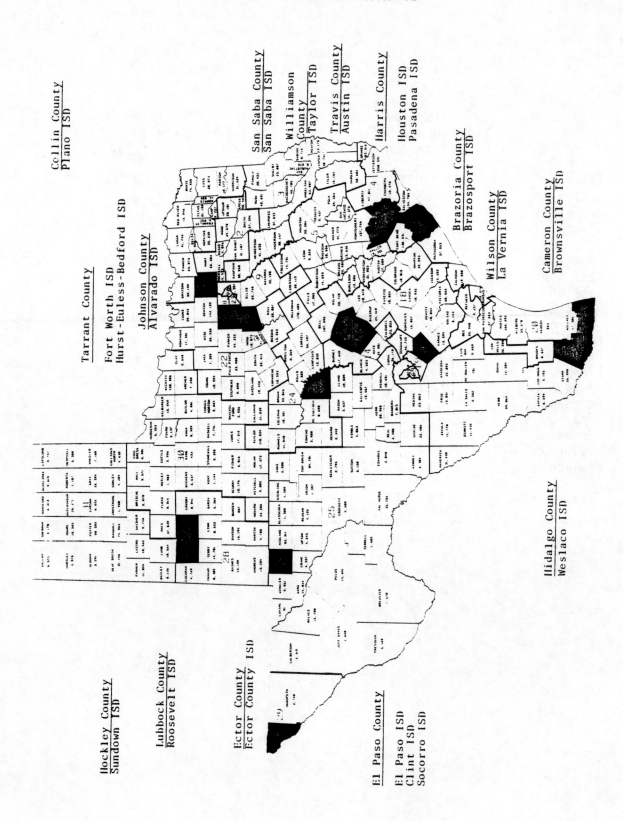

articulate, and eager to improve the quality of education. We were generally impressed with the commitment to education in the districts we observed--a commitment that at times has been sorely tried by a lack of resources (especially in low-wealth districts), by the persistent attacks on education of the past several years, and by derogatory comments from the Select Committee on Public Education and the Texas legislature. There is, we feel, a delicate balance to maintain: even when educational reforms are necessary, it is important not to undermine the morale of teachers and administrators. The dedication of the education community is a resource for the people of Texas, a resource that should at every opportunity be supported and encouraged rather than undermined and degraded.

THE ENDURING DILEMMAS OF EDUCATIONAL REFORM

Because House Bill 72 was such a comprehensive bill, it raises many difficult educational issues. On the whole, we found that most administrators and teachers applauded the reforms of House Bill 72, even when they disagreed with some of its components.[17] But inevitably, in an institution as complex as education, reform is slow and sometimes uncertain. We have therefore examined not only the successes of House Bill 72, but also areas where controversies and problems persist.

Implementation

One initial issue involves the early implementation of House Bill 72. The legislation was signed in July 1984, and revisions in financing and many (although by no means all) programmatic changes started with the 1984-85 school year, which began less than two months after the bill's passage. Administrators therefore had to make changes quickly, in an atmosphere of uncertainty about the legislation itself, with inconsistent interpretations by the Texas Education Agency and uncertainty about what the State Board of Education (SBOE) would do. One issue that comes up consistently, therefore, is how districts have implemented the requirements of House Bill 72 into place and whether this process could have been made smoother.

The Effectiveness of State Legislation

In the area of education, states have three different mechanisms they can use to modify what remains a local activity. They can use financial assistance to districts to encourage some practices over others; they can develop prescriptions requiring districts to follow certain practices; and they can provide technical assistance in the form of information on how to improve educational practices, workshops to train teachers and administrators, consultation about specific problems, and dissemination of information about model programs. House Bill 72 included both financial assistance and prescription, sometimes in coordination and sometimes not.

The crucial question is how effective these mechanisms embodied in House Bill 72 will be in achieving the goals of equity and improved educational quality. Of course, many effects of House Bill 72 will not be known for several years, as districts continue reacting to new requirements and as different provisions are phased in. Still, it is important to begin the assessment of how successful House Bill 72 is likely to be.

State versus Local Control

While House Bill 72 is some way provided school districts greater freedom, by and large this bill (and House Bill 246) increased state control over district practices. House Bill 72 also reconstituted the State Board of Education and strengthened its power, creating a more effective board but also another source of state control. The movement toward state control has been a long-term process in this country; it has been part of the shift toward greater state funding, and periods of reform have also tended to centralize control over education as a way of minimizing variation in educational quality.

Despite the long-term trend toward state control, the question remains whether this trend has gone too far. The shift away from local control may weaken the ability of districts to formulate policies appropriate to local conditions, as well as weakening the initiative and creativity of districts. This is particularly the case if state direction itself is inconsistent, uncertain, or incompetent. A crucial question, therefore, is whether the drift towards greater state control in Texas is appropriate or whether more local control would be more effective in some areas.

Notes

[1]Robert M. Hutchins, The Conflict in Education in a Democratic Society (1954; reprinted, Homewood, Ill.: Greenwood Press, 1972), 71.

[2]U.S. Commission on Civil Rights, Racial Isolation in the Public Schools (Washington, D.C.: U.S. Government Printing Office, 1967).

[3]W. Norton Grubb and Stephen Michaelson, States and Schools: The Political Economy of Public School Finance (Lexington, Mass.: Lexington Books, 1974), Chapter 1.

[4]James W. Guthrie, "United States School Finance Policy, 1955-1980," Educational Evaluation and Policy Analysis 5, no. 2 (Summer 1983): 213.

[5]For a compendium of school finance cases see the series entitled "Update on State-Wide School Finance Cases," published periodically by the Lawyers' Committee for Civil Rights under Law, Washington, D.C.

[6]Stephen B. Thomas and Billy Don Walker, "Texas Public School Finance," Journal of Education Finance 8 (Fall 1982): 223-81.

[7]House Study Group, "The June 1984 Special Session: A Preview," Special Legislative Report no. 103, June 4, 1984, 6.

[8]Guthrie, "United States School Finance Policy," 214-17.

[9]Allan Odden, "Financing Educational Excellence," Phi Delta Kappan 65 (January 1984): 315-16.

[10]See, for example, the summary and critique of several commission reports of the early 1970s in Michael Timpane, Susan Abramowitz, Sue Berryman Bobrow, and Anthony Pascal, Youth Policy in Transition, Report R-2006-HEW (Santa Monica: Rand, 1976).

[11]House Study Group, "Key Issues of the June 1984 Special Session," Special Legislative Report no. 104, July 16, 1984.

[12]House Study Group, "The June 1984 Special Session," 7.

[13]Select Committee on Public Education, Recommendations, April 19, 1984.

[14]For a fuller discussion of the genesis of House Bill 72, see the Texas Association of School Boards, "Legislative Report," for June 8, June 15, June 22, June 29, and July 6, 1984.

[15]For comparisons of reforms in other states, see Thomas Timar, Rules of Reform, manuscript in progress, Institute for Research on Educational Finance and Governance, Stanford University.

[16]Interviews in three other districts were canceled at the last minute because of a statewide snowstorm in February 1985. Of the districts we initially contacted, only one refused to participate, when administrators learned we planned to interview representatives of teacher groups. Administrators in one other district did not return our phone calls attempting to set up interviews. Both these districts were in the San Antonio area, which explains the lack of any interviews in that region. Districts were chosen with the help of David Thompson of the Texas Association of School Boards.

[17]Most of our findings, including the positive attitude of most educators, are corroborated in a study of districts in the San Antonio area; see Nicholas DeLuca, "An Investigation of the Initial Impact of House Bill 72 on the School Districts of Bexar County," Education Council of the Greater San Antonio Chamber of Commerce (February 1985). This report is the only other study we have found on the effects of House Bill 72.

CHAPTER ONE
MOVING TOWARD EQUITY:
THE FINANCING PROVISIONS OF HOUSE BILL 72

In many ways, the heart and soul of House Bill 72 are the changes it made in state aid to districts. These changes included a substantial increase in aid, about 26 percent, from about $3.6 billion in 1983-84 to $4.5 billion in 1984-85.[1] The desire for additional state revenues, originally intended to increase teacher salaries, was in a sense the reason why House Bill 72 as the whole came to be: the need to justify a tax increase for education led to the creation of the Select Committee on Public Education, and SCOPE in turn recommended other reforms adopted in House Bill 72.

House Bill 72 also revised the formulas by which state revenue is distributed, in order to move one step closer to equitable spending patterns. These revisions, responding to a decade of lawsuits and legislative pressures to provide greater equalization among rich and poor districts, were controversial, because in relative terms they redistributed state aid from wealthy districts to poor districts. Only in concert with an overall increase in aid that limited the number of districts which lost state revenue in absolute terms could such a redistribution have been legislated.

The financing of education was changed by House Bill 72 in many other ways. It provided revenues for reforms like the career ladder and for new programs like prekindergarten. The funding of special programs--including compensatory education, bilingual education, and special education for handicapped children--was substantially revised, as we examine further in chapters 4 through 7.

But the most crucial aspect of the finance revisions remains the equalization effort. The equalization issue has been around a long time, and it has been resistant to reform; many of the states that changed their state programs during the 1970s, in response to Serrano v. Priest and other lawsuits, did not produce dramatic improvements in equalization.[2] Still, one important measure of House Bill 72 is its effect on expenditure patterns. As we interviewed educators in districts around the state, we were impressed--or depressed--by the differences wealth can make. Wealthy districts can do anything they want: pay high salaries and attract the best teachers, adopt novel programs (like computer-related courses), build new buildings, equip marvelous libraries and labs, and provide an array of special programs. They are generally unconcerned about reforms coming from Austin, because they know they have the resources to accommodate anything that the legislature or the Texas Education Agency might require. Poor districts have none of these advantages. One superintendent in a poor district admitted that he had to hire the "dregs" of the teacher pool, because of low salaries; shortages of teachers, staff, and supplies are perennial, and there can be no experimenting with new programs. Poor districts also lead a precarious life, fearful that new requirements will further stretch their limited budgets. Where wealthy districts are enormously proud of their enterprises, in poor districts there is a sense of making do and getting by. The differences are enormous and, from the viewpoint of children, inexplicable and unfair. Eliminating these disparities remains a worthy goal of state policy.

PATTERNS OF WEALTH AND THEIR CONSEQUENCES

Most of the formulas in House Bill 72 include district property value in determining the state aid a district receives, in order to direct more aid to poor districts than to wealthy districts. Before analyzing these formulas, it is worth examining the patterns of wealth across the state. (The data used are described in an appendix to this chapter.)

Table 1 describes the magnitude of wealth differences across Texas. The 5 percent of pupils in the poorest districts have a property base of less than $57,800 per pupil, only 25 percent of the state average; the 5 percent in the wealthiest districts have a base of more than $407,800 per pupil, or over seven times as much. Because these wealth differences are so enormous, wealthy districts are able to raise substantially more revenue: total expenditures per pupil in 1983-84, prior to House Bill 72, were over twice as high in the wealthiest districts as in the poorest districts. The differences between districts that are only moderately wealthy and moderately poor are still substantial: moderately poor districts average around $2,600 per pupil while moderately wealthy districts spend around $3,750, or nearly 50 percent more.

Table 1
Expenditures and Tax Rates by Wealth, 1983-84

1983 Wealth per Pupil	Proportion of State ADA	Total Expenditures per Pupil	Operating Expenditures per Pupil	Maintenance & Operation Tax Rate
$ 0-$ 57,800	5.3%	$2,530	$2,201	.337
57,800- 111,400	14.3%	2,638	2,638	.445
111,400- 155,500	15.7%	2,529	2,417	.504
155,500- 191,271	14.6%	3,008	2,533	.520
191,271- 245,000	15.0%	3,341	2,703	.522
245,000- 342,500	14.8%	3,756	3,011	.523
342,500- 407,800	14.9%	3,740*	3,049**	.449
Over $407,800	5.3%	5,123	3,906	.440
Statewide Average		$3,299	$2,704	.482

*Without Houston $4,116
**Without Houston $3,200

Wealth also varies somewhat across different regions of the state (see table 2). Districts in the Panhandle are the wealthiest, because of the presence of oil-rich districts, with an average of $306,568 per student. East Texas districts follow closely behind, with an average of $276,938 per pupil. North Central and West Texas districts are close to the state average of $233,984 per student. Central and South Texas, on the other hand, are relatively less wealthy, and South Texas districts, with average property per student of $148,293, are about half as wealthy as districts in the Panhandle.

Table 2
District Characteristics by Region, 1983-84

	Wealth per Pupil	Total Expenditures per Pupil	Percent Black	Percent Hispanic
Panhandle	$306,568	$3,492	7.1%	29.2%
North Central Texas	245,462	3,227	20.9%	12.0%
West Texas	245,162	3,109	3.7%	62.9%
South Texas	148,293	2,938	3.0%	60.9%
Central Texas	198,851	3,246	12.8%	22.8%
East Texas	276,938	3,590	22.6%	15.2%
Statewide Average	$233,984	$3,229	15.8%	26.5%

The distribution of minority groups across the state has several fiscal implications for these students. Hispanics are most heavily concentrated in South and West Texas, and they therefore tend to be concentrated in low-wealth districts with low expenditure levels. Blacks, on the other hand, tend to live in urban areas, which are somewhat wealthier than average because of the presence of commercial and industrial property. As a result, the average Hispanic child lives in a district where expenditures per pupil were $3,071 in 1983-84, somewhat lower than the average of $3,409 for Anglos and $3,316 for black students.

Texas includes a large number of districts--1,068, not including several special districts for military bases, the Texas Youth Commission, and state schools for the mentally retarded--with an enormous range of sizes: the smallest districts in 1983-84 reported an average daily attendance (ADA) of 1.44, while Houston had 171,444 students. As table 3 shows, the smallest districts include many of the oil-rich areas and therefore tend to be wealthy. In general, both the largest and the smallest districts tend to be wealthier than middle-sized districts. However, aside from higher spending per pupil in the very smallest districts, there is no particular relationship between size and expenditures per pupil.

Table 3
District Characteristics by Size of District, 1983-84

Average Daily Attendance	Number of Districts	Percent of State ADA	Average Wealth	Total Expenditures per Pupil
0- 100	85	0.2%	$1,210,733	$6,060
100- 500	376	3.8%	361,245	3,803
500- 1,000	198	5.2%	293,648	3,365
1,000- 1,600	119	5.5%	251,343	3,292
1,600- 3,000	115	9.2%	198,971	3,258
3,000-10,000	115	19.7%	195,488	3,263
10,000-25,000	42	23.9%	206,954	3,376
25,000-50,000	12	13.9%	199,427	3,076
50,000 and over	6	18.4%	295,423	3,280
Statewide Average	1,068	$2,731,019 (ADA)	$ 233,984	$3,299

THE STRUCTURE OF FINANCING UNDER HOUSE BILL 72

Prior to H.B. 72, state aid was granted to districts on the basis of the number of personnel employed. Under the new legislation, state aid is based on the number of students in average daily attendance. The basic allotment for each district is $1,290 per student for 1984-85 and $1,350 per student each year thereafter. This is simply a starting point, however, because so many adjustments are made to the basic allotment in determining a district's aid.

One initial adjustment to the basic allotment is a provision that provides additional aid to small and sparsely populated districts, including all those with an ADA of less than 1,600. (These 787 small districts included only 15 percent of statewide ADA.) This adjustment is far from trivial: a district with an ADA of 800, for example, receives a 20 percent or 32 percent increase, with the higher increase for those districts that are sparsely populated (larger than 300 square miles). The justification for this funding is presumably that some districts suffer from diseconomies of small size.

A second set of adjustments to the basic allotment allows differences in costs from special programs. Each student in compensatory education receives an extra 20 percent of the adjusted basic allotment; each student in a bilingual program receives an extra 10 percent; each vocational student receives an additional 45 percent; and the weights for special education students vary with the instructional arrangement. In the first year of House

Bill 72, compensatory education costs were strongly correlated with the proportion of Hispanic children in school districts and only moderately correlated with the proportion of black children; bilingual funds were correlated with the presence of Hispanic children, as expected, while funds for vocational education and special education were not highly correlated with any particular group. (Appendix table 1 presents correlation coefficients describing these relationships.) Compensatory and bilingual funds were more concentrated in South Texas, because of the presence of Hispanic children in these areas. It appears, then, that these funds are being distributed appropriately among districts.

However, a commonly expressed concern among the educators we interviewed was that the weights in House Bill 72 are inadequate to fund these special programs. Some administrators asserted that the weights were accurate but resulted in insufficient funds when applied to the basic allotment, because the $1,290 allotment itself was too low. In general, the districts felt that the weights do not account for overhead and other related costs, such as facilities and buses. This complaint was mentioned most often in relation to the proposed special education weights; revised weights, generally higher, have been approved by the State Board of Education but not by the state legislature since the passage of House Bill 72.

Price Differential Index

A more complex adjustment to the basic allotment involves the price differential index (PDI). The PDI is a price index intended to reflect the variation among districts in costs of providing education, since the purchasing power of a dollar of state aid is not the same in all districts in a state as large as Texas. Although the desirability of using a price index in calculating state aid has been well known for several decades, only two other states (Florida and Missouri) have adopted a price index, partly because of the technical complexity of such indices and partly because of political resistance. In Texas, there were not only sound economic reasons for using such an index--because of the tremendous variation in costs across the state-- but also political reasons: the coalition of districts that helped pass House Bill 72 included low-wealth districts benefiting from equalization and high-cost urban districts benefiting from the PDI.

For 1983-84, a temporary PDI was devised. For most districts this index included the ratio of the total teacher salaries paid in the previous year in other districts in the same county to the total minimum salary level of the same districts. (This portion of the index is based on the salaries of neighboring districts in order to keep the PDI from acting as an incentive for districts to increase their own salaries.) The salary ratio is then added to .10 times the proportion of a district's students who are "educationally disadvantaged" (i.e., low-income students), to reflect the higher costs of educating these students. The sum is then subject to a maximum and a minimum for the highest and lowest 5 percent of districts and adjusted so that the lowest PDI equals 1. Then a district's basic allotment is increased by 75 percent of the amount by which a district's PDI exceeds 1; for example, a district with a PDI of 1.10 would receive a 7.5 percent increase in its basic allotment.

In 1984-85, the PDI ranged from 1.00 to 1.289, so that it generated an increase of up to 21.7 percent for districts with highest costs. The average PDI was 1.192, so that the average adjusted basic allotment (without considering adjustments for small districts) was $1,476, considerably higher than $1,290. The PDI turns out to be moderately positively correlated with wealth and with size.[3] These patterns seem appropriate, since urban districts have higher costs of living and wealthy districts are likely to have higher land and housing costs. However, there are some curiosities in the index: South Texas, the poorest region, has the highest average PDI (1.218), probably because of the high proportion of low-income students, although it is generally considered a low-cost region. Central Texas has a very low average PDI (1.067), while the other regions are near the state average.

Unavoidably, the initial index adopted by House Bill 72 has generated a great deal of controversy. Almost every district protested the use of teacher salaries as a proxy for resource costs. Finance and budget directors complained about the complexity of the PDI, but they also proclaimed that other variables (e.g., economies of scale, business costs, the cost of living, the district's wealth, and even Mexico's economy for border towns) should be taken into account. The prevalent feeling was that the PDI benefits the large, urban, and wealthy districts more than others.

House Bill 72 specified that a Price Differential Index Committee should be established to develop a more refined PDI. This revised PDI, adopted for 1985-86, is based on variation in ADA, the proportion of low-income students, the county average wage of individuals in private firms and noneducation public agencies, and density (students per square mile).[4] Even before its application, this index has also been criticized for ignoring a variety of other factors that affect costs. In addition, the method of calculation ensures that differences among districts will be as small as possible, so that this index probably undercorrects for price differences.[5] Still further revisions to the PDI are being proposed, and it is likely that this part of House Bill 72 will remain controversial.

The Equalizing Mechanism of House Bill 72

House Bill 72 operates by calculating a basic allotment for each district, including adjustments for special programs, small districts, and the PDI. In general, this amount should not have an equalizing effect; in fact, because the PDI is correlated with wealth, this amount would also be higher for wealthy districts. The equalizing power of House Bill 72 comes from the calculation of the "local share," an amount which is higher for wealthy districts than for poor districts. The amount of state aid, then, is the adjusted basic allotment minus the local share, an amount that is substantially higher for poor districts.

The local share is calculated so that the state funds 70 percent of the statewide costs associated with the adjusted basic allotment plus transportation aid, falling to 67.7 percent in 1985-86 and thereafter. Its equalizing effect comes from the fact that the local share depends on the ratio of district property value per pupil to statewide property value per pupil. Thus, the wide disparities in property values shown in table 1 affect the calculation of aid.

Table 4 illustrates this equalizing mechanism. The amount per pupil of the foundation school program cost does not vary significantly by wealth of district. However, the local share is much higher for wealthy districts, so state aid per pupil from this component of House Bill 72 is higher for poor districts--more than three times as much per pupil for the poorest pupils as for the wealthiest ones.

Table 4
The Equalizing Mechanism of House Bill 72

Wealth per Pupil	Total Foundation School Program Cost	Local Cost per Pupil	State Cost per Pupil
$ 0- 57,800	$1,911	$ 129	$1,862
57,800-111,400	1,933	231	1,703
111,400-155,500	1,896	341	1,555
155,500-191,271	1,853	448	1,405
191,271-245,000	1,896	565	1,331
245,000-342,500	1,928	742	1,186
342,500-407,800	1,980	969	1,011
Over $407,800	2,048	1,456	592
Statewide Average	$1,925	$ 578	$1,350

The equalizing mechanism of House Bill 72 will become slightly stronger in 1985-86, largely because the local share increases from 30 percent to 33.3 percent of the total foundation school program in the state. This change will in effect increase the importance of differences in property value in calculating state aid. In light of our findings (presented later in this chapter) that wealth-based inequalities in expenditures per pupil remain substantial, even after the changes of House Bill 72, the strengthening of the equalizing effect seems appropriate.

Enrichment Equalization Allotment

Yet another mechanism of equalization in House Bill 72 is the enrichment equalization allotment (EEA), which provides a special incentive for districts of moderate and low wealth to increase their local tax rates to "enrich" their educational offerings. Only districts with wealth per student less than 110 percent of the statewide average ($248,185 in this analysis) receive EEA. The maximum aid per student is 35 percent of the district's other foundation school allocation in 1984-85, but this maximum aid is adjusted according to property value per pupil so that low-wealth districts receive more than high-wealth districts. The incentive effect of EEA is due to the fact that aid increases as a district's tax rate increases (subject to a maximum), so that a 10 percent increase in the local rate increases EEA aid by 10 percent.[6]

During interviews, several administrators criticized equalization enrichment aid because its calculation does not include the tax rate supporting capital expenditures. However, this comment appears to be due to a misunderstanding about the EEA formula, which does allow districts to use their total tax (rather than their tax rate for operating expenditures only) in calculating their EEA. In fact, this is the only provision in H.B. 72 that provides any state aid because of capital and interest costs; the lack of any other funding for debt service and capital expenditures is discussed later in this chapter.

Of the 1,068 school districts in Texas, 720 received equalization aid in 1984-85. The average wealth for these districts was $158,710 per pupil, 64 percent of the statewide average wealth per pupil. As table 5 indicates, the amount of equalization enrichment aid is strongly related to wealth. Therefore, this form of aid does have a strong equalizing effect as intended, although the amounts of aid are much smaller than aid from the state's share of the foundation school programs.

Table 5
Other Components of State Aid by District Wealth

Wealth per pupil	Enrichment Equalization Allotment	Experienced Teacher Allotment	Equalization Transition Entitlement
$ 0- 57,800	$440	$104	$ 0
57,800-111,400	368	65	0
111,400-155,500	290	39	0
155,500-191,271	195	30	0
191,271-245,000	87	26	10
245,000-342,500	2	27	36
342,500-407,800	0	54	37
Over $407,800	0	30	224
Statewide Average	$164	$ 43	$ 24

Among the regions of Texas, South Texas receives the highest equalization enrichment allotment per pupil, $281, because of its low average property value; the West Texas region is second with $257 (as table 6 indicates). East Texas receives the least amount of equalization aid, $91 per pupil. Again because of patterns of wealth, districts with high proportions of Hispanic children tend to receive more EEA, while those with high proportions of black students tend to receive less.

Table 6
Other Components of State Aid by Region

	Enrichment Equalization Allotment	Experienced Teacher Allotment	Equalization Transition Entitlement
Panhandle	$214	$39	$30
North Central Texas	120	28	24
West Texas	257	60	18
South Texas	281	74	18
Central Texas	177	35	18
East Texas	91	33	18
Statewide Average	$164	$43	$24

The enrichment equalization aid formula stipulates that the maximum entitlement will be reduced from 35 percent to 30 percent beginning in the 1985-86 school year and continuing thereafter. This change will reduce the incentive for moderate- and low-wealth districts to increase their tax rates, so that both local revenues in these districts and state EEA will decline,[7] The result will be to dilute slightly the equalizing effects of House Bill 72.

The Experienced Teacher Allotment

House Bill 72 also provided an experienced teacher allotment (ETA), intended to compensate partially those districts with many experienced teachers for their higher salary costs. One component of the ETA is based on the ratio of the district's property value per pupil to the state average property value per pupil, so that poor districts might receive more ETA. Another component of the ETA formula is in effect based on the ratio of the district's average minimum teacher salary to that of the state as a whole, so that districts that have more experienced teachers than average (and thus a higher average minimum teacher salary) receive more ETA. Districts therefore have an incentive to hire more experienced teachers, an incentive which is greater for poor districts. In fact, districts with experience levels below the state average receive no ETA.

In one sense, the ETA components are potentially contradictory. The equalizing component implies that poor districts should get more ETA, but as wealthier districts can more readily afford to hire experienced teachers, the second component could lead to poor districts receiving relatively less ETA. In fact, the two effects almost cancel each other out: table 5 shows that, while the poorest districts do tend to receive slightly more ETA, the differences by wealth are not especially large.

However, other patterns for ETA emerged from the data. One is that districts with high proportions of Hispanic pupils receive more ETA. ETA is also positively correlated with the proportion of blacks and with district size, although more moderately. Evidently, these districts tend to have more experienced teachers and thus qualify for more ETA.

The average ETA in the state was only $43 per pupil, a rather modest sum compared to other provisions of House Bill 72. Perhaps because of the small amount of aid, many districts surveyed (both those receiving and those not receiving ETA) reported that this provision would not affect hiring practices at all. Most personnel officers contend that they hire the best people they can, regardless of the aid. Many showed a desire to promote teachers from within a district, rather than trying to hire experienced teachers from outside the district. It seems likely that this provision of House Bill 72 is relatively ineffective as a stimulus to districts, although it has tended to help those districts with unavoidably higher costs because of experienced teachers.

Equalization Transition Entitlement

The equalization transition entitlement (ETE) was designed to moderate the effects of House Bill 72 for those very wealthy districts whose state aid was reduced for the years 1984-85 through 1986-87. ETE replaces part of the loss in state aid per pupil over the previous year--60 percent of the loss in 1984-85, 40 percent in 1985-86, and 20 percent in 1986-87. After 1987, ETE will no longer be in effect. A district's entitlement is adjusted for tax effort, so that a higher tax rate generates more ETE, providing an incentive to keep tax rates up. In fact, another provision in the ETE formula provides for a reduction in ETE: if a district's tax levy does not increase enough to make up the unreimbursed shortfall in state aid between one year and the next, then ETE is reduced, providing still another incentive for these very wealthy districts to keep their tax rates high.

In 1984-85, 25 percent of all districts (272), which include 23 percent of all students, received transition aid. These districts receive an average of $114 per pupil, although the wealthiest districts received about twice this amount (see tables 5 and 6). The average wealth of this group is $441,557, 1.8 times the statewide average. As table 5 clarifies, all ETE goes to districts above the median wealth level, and about half goes to the wealthiest 5 percent of districts. Since the purpose of transition aid is to soften the blow of reductions in foundation state aid, this pattern is not surprising. However, ETE does undermine the equalizing intent of the rest of House Bill 72.

No other strong patterns of ETE emerge. There is a weak tendency for East Texas and Panhandle districts to receive more than other regions, and for districts with high proportions of both black and Hispanic students to receive somewhat less, but these differences are not particularly large.

Other Provisions of House Bill 72 with Fiscal Implications

The funding formulas reviewed above generate the majority of revenues to school districts. However, there are numerous other measures in House Bill 72 that affect the financing of public education, some accompanied by state revenues and some of them requiring that districts must fund from local revenues.

House Bill 72 requires that districts establish a career ladder for teachers and administrators. The career ladder, analyzed more fully in the next section of this chapter and in chapter 2, is funded by a grant of $100 per pupil, $30 of which must be used for salary supplements required by the career ladder.

Another requirement is that districts with at least fifteen eligible children must offer a prekindergarten program for low-income or limited English proficiency children, beginning in 1985-86. This program is partly funded by the state, with a $36.3 million appropriation for 1985-86 and $45 million for 1986-87; the state's share is higher for poor districts than for wealthy districts, so that differences in the abilities of poor and wealthy districts to fund prekindergarten programs will be somewhat reduced. Districts with bilingual education will be required to offer a summer bilingual preschool program beginning in the summer of 1985, with a separate state appropriation of $5.7 million. These two preschool programs are analyzed in greater detail in chapter 8.

Finally, House Bill 72 prescribes a maximum class size of twenty-two for kindergarten, first, and second grades beginning in 1985-86; this ratio will apply to third and fourth grades beginning in 1988-89. These provisions will require many districts to hire new teachers and build new classrooms, although these additional costs will not be supported by the state. The consequences for districts, and the potential hardships for poor districts, are analyzed below.

A number of school district administrators, some from average-sized and average-wealth districts, indicated concern about the burden imposed by requiring but not funding (or not funding fully) the maximum class size and the prekindergarten and summer bilingual programs. Several districts predicted that additional bond issues would be necessary to support construction of new facilities. Other districts indicated that a tax rate increase would be necessary, while another district said it would use state compensatory education funds for a prekindergarten and summer bilingual program. However districts plan to meet these requirements, it appears that new programs and requirements without state support generate some fiscal stress within districts, at least for those of low and moderate wealth.

THE INITIAL EFFECTS OF HOUSE BILL 72 ON SALARIES AND EXPENDITURES

The complete effects of House Bill 72 will not be known for several years, as different changes in the legislation begin to take effect and as districts continue to adjust to the new financing mechanisms. Nonetheless, it is valuable to examine the initial effects of House Bill 72 on expenditures in 1984-85, to see if these effects are consistent with the intent of the legislation. The results in this section are based on a survey administered in the fall of 1984, by the Texas Association of School Boards and the Texas Association of School Administrators. (An appendix to this chapter describes these data more fully.) Therefore, the findings in this section represent the reported plans of school districts for expenditures in 1984-85, rather than final expenditures.

Effects on Salaries

One fundamental purpose of increased state aid was to increase the salaries of public school employees, especially teachers. As summarized in table 7, districts reported that teacher salaries averaged $20,426 in 1983-84 and $22,455 in 1984-85, an increase of $2,029 or nearly 10 percent.[8] This increase was somewhat higher than the growth rate of salaries in private employment, estimated to be about 6.6 percent for 1984.[9] Since inflation has been about 3.5 percent over the past year, the increase in real or inflation-adjusted teacher salaries was about 6.5 percent. Surprisingly, this was not necessarily greater than increases that have occurred in the past. In 1982-83 teacher salaries increased 11.5 percent over the previous year, a real increase of 7.2 percent; the increase in 1981-82 was 11.8 percent (a real increase of 5.6 percent), and the increase in 1980-81 was 11.3 percent (a real increase of 2.6 percent).[10]

However, salary increases were not evenly spread among teachers. The TASB/TASA survey asked districts to report their lowest, average, and highest teacher salaries to give some idea of the range of salaries being paid within districts. In 1983-84, the average low salary was $14,198, and this increased 22 percent to $17,341 in 1984-85. However, the reported average salary increased by only 12 percent, from $20,335 to $22,800;[11] and the reported highest teacher salary increased by 8.5 percent, from $28,331 to $30,742. This indicates that salaries of beginning teachers and those with little experience have increased much more than moderate and high salaries, tending to compress salary differentials within districts. These results corroborate some results from interviews in a sample of districts, analyzed at a greater length in chapter 2: teachers and administrators have indicated that House Bill 72 provided a considerable boost to starting teacher salaries, but did less to increase salaries for more experienced teachers.

One provision of House Bill 72 designed to increase starting salaries is

----

Table 7
Salaries and Expenditures in Texas School Districts

	Unweighted		Weighted	
	1983-84	1984-85	1983-84	1984-85
Teachers	$18,190	$20,957	$20,426	$22,455
Administrators	23,228	35,253	32,156	35,329
Other Professionals	19,860	22,509	23,818	25,372
Paraprofessionals/				
Clericals	9,507	10,413	10,486	11,176
Auxiliary	7,539	8,214	9,251	10,049
Low Teacher Salary	12,920	16,613	14,198	17,341
Average Teacher Salary	18,228	21,040	20,335	22,800
High Teacher Salary	24,575	27,601	28,331	30,742
Operating Expenditure				
per Student	2,800	3,274	2,581	2,827

----

the minimum salary of $15,200, a 37 percent increase over the previous minimum of $11,100. Of the 667 districts that provided information on their lowest salaries, 137 (or about 20 percent) reported paying starting teachers exactly $15,200. Those at the minimum are generally small districts, since only 9 of these district have enrollments over 3,000. Although the direct influence of the minimum salary is limited to only one-fifth of the districts, its indirect influence is much greater, because many districts try to keep their salaries well above the minimum as a way of attracting more teachers.

Other district personnel also received substantial salary increases in 1984-85. Statewide salaries for administrators increased from an average of $32,156 in 1983-84 to $35,329 in 1984-85, a 10 percent increase comparable to the increase that teachers received. Other personnel received somewhat lower increases. Paraprofessional and clerical salaries rose from $10,486 to $11,176, an increase of 6.6 percent; average salaries for auxiliary employees (like janitors and food service workers) increased 8.6 percent, from $9,251 to $10,049; and salaries of other professional personnel (like counselors and librarians) increased 8 percent, from $23,818 to $25,732. Therefore, teachers and administrators received the highest proportional salary increases, while paraprofessional, clerical, and auxiliary employees received lower relative increases. Salary growth outpaced the 3.5 percent inflation rate for all groups and was generally greater than the average salary increase of 6.6 percent projected for the private sector.

The Career Ladder

An important change in House Bill 72 was the establishment of a career ladder for teachers, providing a supplement of up to $2,000 for some teachers selected on the basis of merit. As the career ladder continues to be one of the most controversial aspects of House Bill 72, information about its operation is of special interest.

Of the 679 districts responding to the TASB/TASA questionnaire, only one third (or less) responded to questions about the career ladder. The others reported that they had not yet made any decisions about the career ladder, and many reported that they were waiting for guidelines from the State Board of Education. The finding that the majority of districts had not made any decisions about the career ladder by the fall of 1984 corroborates our evidence from interviewing in districts, where we discovered a great deal of uncertainty and confusion about the career ladder. The low response rate to questions about the career ladder means that our results are subject to considerable error and should be interpreted only as suggestive.

House Bill 72 provides procedures for determining how many teachers are eligible for level II of the career ladder and then allows districts to promote all or only some of those eligible. Those districts who responded to these questions reported that 56 percent of their teachers would be eligible for the career ladder in 1984-85. Of those eligible, districts planned to promote 71 percent to level II. This suggests that almost 34 percent of all teachers would be promoted to level II during this school year. However, these averages may be misleading because of large variation among districts. For example, 13 percent of districts reported that they would promote one-third or less of eligible teachers to level II, while 29 percent reported they would promote all eligible teachers. This variation appears to reflect the exercise of considerable discretion among districts. While larger districts report that they will promote a slightly lower proportion of eligible teachers, there is no tendency for wealthy districts to promote more.

House Bill 72 presumes that districts will provide a salary supplement of $2,000 to every teacher promoted on the career ladder, unless the state allotments to fund the career ladder are insufficient; the supplements can then be reduced to $1,500. Of the districts that responded, 169 (or 59 percent) planned to provide a supplement of $1,500 while only 81 (28 percent) planned to offer the full $2,000; the remaining districts planned to give a supplement between $1,500 and $2,000. The amount of the supplement is not, surprisingly, related to wealth; if anything, there is a slight tendency for wealth to be negatively correlated with the supplement. Large districts tend to have lower supplements, possibly because they have higher salaries to begin with.

Based on this information, it appears that the state aid for the career ladder is insufficient in most districts to fund the career ladder fully, since most districts are providing less than the full $2,000 supplement. However, the adequacy of funding for the career ladder is a tricky issue.

House Bill 72 provides $100 per pupil for an educational improvement and career ladder allotment, and requires that at least $30 per pupil of that amount be spent on the career ladder itself in 1984-85; however, districts could spend an additional $35 per pupil of the career ladder allotment on the career ladder, as well as local revenues. From interviews with school district administrators, it appears that most districts are using just $30 per pupil to fund the career ladder, with the remaining $70 per pupil going to other purposes permitted by House Bill 72. Apparently, then, the required $30 per pupil is insufficient to fund the career ladder fully, while $100 per pupil might be sufficient (at least in the first years of House Bill 72, when only level II is relevant).

The TASB/TASA survey also asked districts whether they have any other incentive pay plan. Of the 615 districts that responded to this question, 99 (or 16 percent) reported that they had some other incentive plan. These districts tend to be substantially larger than districts without their own plan. They report that they plan to promote 74 percent of eligible teachers to level II, while those without their own plans will promote 64 percent, suggesting that districts with their own incentive plans are more willing to use the career ladder as well. There seem to be no other marked differences between these two groups of districts, although there is a small correlation between wealth and the existence of an incentive pay plan.[12]

Because our results for career ladder plans are based on so few responses, they may not be conclusive. However, they do suggest that it would be valuable to monitor district plans for the career ladder as these plans become more firmly established.

Operating Expenditures

The districts responding to the TASB/TASA questionnaire reported that operating expenditures per pupil averaged $2,827 in 1984-85, compared to a 1983-84 figure of $2,581.[13] Therefore, state average expenditures per pupil increased about 9.5 percent.

Teacher salaries represented 49 percent of total expenditures in 1984-85. Paraprofessional and clerical salaries represented 7 percent; administrators and auxiliary personnel salaries each accounted for another 8 percent; and other professional personnel salaries accounted for 4 percent. Collectively, these five categories of personnel cost accounted for almost 77 percent of total operating budgets. Teacher salaries in 1984-85 are a somewhat higher fraction than they were the previous year, when they constituted 46.5 percent of current operating expenditure. Thus, the major effect of House Bill 72 has been to increase expenditures generally, with spending on teachers receiving a small extra increase.

Additional Costs: The Effects of Minimum Class Size

House Bill 72 requires districts to meet a maximum class size of twenty-two pupils for kindergarten through second grade, beginning in the 1985-86 school year. This will require some districts to hire new teachers and to provide more classrooms for these smaller classes. Of the 623 districts that reported how many additional teachers they would need, 19 percent reported that they would need none; another 57 percent indicated a need for one to five teachers, and 24 percent responded that they would need more than five teachers. A few large districts account for the bulk of the 3,872 total extra teachers that districts said they would need: Houston reported that it would need 557; Fort Worth, 175; Corpus Christ, 137; El Paso, 155; and Austin, 104.

Overall, the number of additional teachers needed amounts to an average increase of 3.3 percent in total teachers (for all grade levels) in the reporting districts. However, the need for teachers will be higher in low-spending districts.   Those spending less than the median expenditure per pupil reported that they would require an average of 3.6 percent more teachers, while high-spending districts will require an average of 2.7 percent more. The reason is simply that high-spending districts usually have lower pupil/teacher ratios already, and thus more of them are already under the maximum class size or are relatively close to it.

The requirement of smaller classes will also cause many districts to build new classrooms. Almost 40 percent of districts indicated that they had unused classrooms available to absorb all or part of the additional classes required; 31 percent responded that they would not need to build any additional classrooms. The other 69 percent of districts reported that they would have to add another 3,388 classrooms. (Not surprisingly, the number of additional classrooms necessary is only slightly less than the number of additional teachers necessary, and the number of additional classrooms a district needs is highly correlated with the number of additional teachers.) The six largest districts account for about one-third of these. The burden of building new classrooms again seems to fall more heavily on low-spending districts: the ratio of new classrooms per existing teacher--a crude measure of the relative increase in classrooms--was 3 percent for low-spending districts but 2.5 percent for high-spending districts. Evidently, high-spending districts tend to have smaller classes already and will be less likely to need to build new classrooms.

The need for additional teachers and classrooms broken down by pupil/teacher ratios shows a clear pattern: as the existing pupil/teacher ratio increases, the need for additional teachers and classrooms increases (see table 8). The need for additional pupils and teachers is especially great in those districts with the highest pupil/teacher ratios. Many of the districts with higher pupil/teacher ratios are larger districts; conversely, many of the districts with low ratios are small rural districts that often don't have enough pupils in every grade to have large class sizes.   At the same time, districts that already have higher ratios and greater need for additional teachers and classrooms tend to have lower property values as well, while districts with low pupil/teacher ratios and lower needs for more teachers and classrooms tend to be wealthier.

Table 8
Wealth Per Pupil and Additional Costs by Pupil/Teacher Ratio

Pupil/Teacher Ratio	Wealth	Additional Teachers	Additional Classrooms
Less Than/Equal to 13:1	$577,720	1.135	1.079
Greater Than 13:1, Less Than/Equal to 16:1	$352,280	2.771	2.731
Greater Than 16:1, Less Than/Equal to 17:1	$213,481	5.636	6.323
Greater Than 17:1	$245,039	13.826	11.600

Under House Bill 72, the cost of decreasing the class size to twenty-two must come entirely from local revenues, because state aid increases only as average daily attendance increases and not when ADA is fixed and the number of teachers increases. Similarly, all capital costs are paid wholly by local funds, since Texas has no state aid for capital outlays. Thus, the costs of meeting the maximum class size will come wholly from local revenues and will fall somewhat more heavily on low-spending, low-wealth districts that are least able to raise local revenue.

Equalization

A major purpose of House Bill 72 was to equalize district expenditures within the state of Texas--that is, to narrow the gap between the expenditures of wealthy, high-spending districts and low-wealth, low-spending districts. The current operating expenditures reported to TASB/TASA indicate that inequalities in spending have been reduced. As table 9 indicates, spending in the wealthiest districts in 1983-84 averaged $3,667--$1,605 per pupil, or 78 percent more than the average of $2,062 spent in the poorest districts. In 1984-85, the spending advantage of the wealthiest districts had fallen to 44 percent, or $1,173 per pupil. Similarly, the advantage of the near-wealthiest districts over the near-poorest fell from $715 per pupil, or 34 percent in 1983-84 to $616, or 25 percent, in 1984-85. These findings are similar to the results using TEA's data on expenditures per pupil, presented in appendix table 2. (The spending differences are larger in TEA data than in the TASB/TASA data because the latter omit some small, wealthy, high-spending districts.)

Similarly, the gap between teacher salaries in rich and poor districts, which determine their ability to hire good teachers, fell in 1984-85. The difference between the wealthiest and the poorest districts in average teacher

----

Table 9
Changes in Teacher Salaries and Expenditures by Wealth

Wealth per Pupil	Low Teacher Salary		Average Teacher Salary	
	1983-84	1984-85	1983-84	1984-85
$ 0- 57,800	$12,113	$17,023	$17,195	$21,378
57,800-111,400	12,241	16,189	17,246	20,336
111,400-155,500	12,335	16,559	18,336	21,295
155,500-191,271	13,774	17,361	20,215	23,053
191,271-245,000	14,283	17,379	20,624	23,104
245,000-342,500	15,158	17,929	21,613	23,850
342,500-407,800	16,145	18,271	22,186	23,898
Over $407,800	15,568	18,262	21,849	24,296
Statewide Average	$14,165	$17,391	$20,278	$22,768

Wealth per Pupil	Operating Expenditures per Pupil	
	1983-84	1984-85
$ 0- 57,800	$ 2,062	$ 2,674
57,800-111,400	2,126	2,440
111,400-155,550	2,276	2,451
155,500-191,271	2,389	2,776
191,271-245,000	2,525	2,786
245,000-342,500	2,831	3,142
342,500-407,800	2,841*	3,056**
Over $407,800	3,667	3,847
Statewide Average	$ 2,537	$ 2,851

*Without Houston $2,975
**Without Houston $3,228

----

salaries was $4,654 in 1983-84 and fell to $2,918 in 1984-85. The gap in beginning teacher salaries fell from $3,455 to $1,235, a larger reduction in both absolute and relative terms. Thus, House Bill 72 has done more to equalize starting teacher salaries than to equalize either average teacher salaries or overall expenditures per pupil.

There are many other ways to show the relationships among wealth, expenditures per pupil, and teacher salaries, but they all generate the same conclusion. In the first year after House Bill 72, both expenditure differences and differences in teacher salaries between rich and poor districts have narrowed, but not vanished. No matter how the data are analyzed, substantial differences remain between rich and poor districts.[14]

Of course, it may be that districts have not fully adjusted their expenditures to the new state aid patterns of House Bill 72. If wealthy districts have adjusted their expenditures while poor districts have not, this would tend to dampen the equalizing effects of House Bill 72, which gives much more aid to low-wealth districts than was previously the case. Unless this effect is powerful, however, it appears that House Bill 72 has been only moderately successful in equalizing expenditures and teacher salaries.

CONCLUSIONS: THE CONTINUING PROBLEMS OF FINANCING SCHOOLS IN TEXAS

In many ways, the financing changes introduced by House Bill 72 have been successful, even in the first year. Teacher salaries increased substantially, especially for beginning teachers. The increase in state aid has slightly shifted the funding of schools away from the local property tax--the most disliked of all major taxes--toward state taxes.[15] In a state where equalization has been a constant source of concern over the past decade, House Bill 72 reduced the disparities in expenditures and teacher salaries between the poor and wealthy districts somewhat.

House Bill 72 also made a series of other, smaller changes in specific programs. The increases in funds for compensatory education, bilingual education, and education for handicapped children--analyzed in chapters 4, 5, and 6--have been welcomed by advocates for these groups of children. The changes in funding for vocational education--examined in chapter 7--are more controversial, although they have the potential to reduce the high costs of these programs.

There are many other changes whose effects cannot yet be evaluated. The career ladder is one of these: although funding for the career ladder was a miniscule portion of House Bill 72, the controversy over this provision has been enormous, and its effects on teacher quality will not be evident for several years. Similarly, the requirements for prekindergarten programs and summer preschool programs have led districts to begin planning for them, although the quality and effectiveness of these novel programs will again be unknown for several years.

In the 1985 legislative session, no changes were made to the funding provisions of House Bill 72. Despite the fact that a revenue shortage developed and many legislators wanted to curtail school funding to increase expenditures in other areas, the supporters of House Bill 72 managed to keep its funding intact. However, it became equally clear that the schools of Texas can anticipate no new funding in the near future. Both the 1983 and the 1985 legislative sessions had to wrestle with revenue shortages, and these are unlikely to disappear. The long-term prospects for oil and gas severance taxes, which in the past have provided about 1/4 percent of state revenues, are dismal, and Texas has a tax structure which is relatively unresponsive to economic growth.[16] As a result, it is likely that new funds will be available for schools only if new taxes or tax increases are enacted.

As a result, the deficiencies in House Bill 72 are likely to remain for some time. There are several provisions of the legislation that have been applauded but that educators feel are inadequately funded. For example, teacher salaries increased because of House Bill 72, but experienced teachers generally complain that their increases have been too small. Educators have welcomed the increased funding for bilingual education, compensatory education, and special education, but the demands on these funds are increasing--especially with declines in federal revenues--so these programs still seem underfunded. The revenues designated for the career ladder seem inadequate to fund it at the level the legislature deemed appropriate. In general, many commentators feel that the basic allotment, which averaged $1,919 per pupil after adjustments, was too low in a state where the average expenditure per pupil is about $2,800. However, the increases in state funding that these complaints imply are unlikely to materialize without a tax increase. Despite this fact of political reality, it is worth outlining several problems that House Bill 72 has helped create, and that will continue to trouble school financing in Texas until new state revenues materialize.

State Funding and State Requirements

The State of Texas can influence local educational practice either through funding or through the requirements it imposes on local districts. House Bill 72 contains both kinds of provisions, of course, but the two mechanisms are not always coordinated. There are several cases of requirements without funds. The maximum class size of twenty-two in kindergarten through grade two is one example; such a requirement forces some districts to come up with local revenues to pay for more teachers and more classrooms. Since poor districts are more likely to have overcrowded classrooms, this requirement results in a heavier burden on them than on wealthy districts. The interaction of House Bill 246 and House Bill 72 provides another example: House Bill 246 required changes in curriculum without funding, and administrators admit that they were forced to use revenues from House Bill 72 to finance the curriculum changes of House Bill 246. The tutorials required by House Bill 72 are another example: since the tutorials are not specifically funded, many districts are using state compensatory education funds, although these funds are not necessarily calculated to cover the costs of tutorials and other forms of remediation.

In subsequent years, districts will face additional requirements from House Bill 72, yet state funding will not increase as it did in 1984-85. On the contrary, for many districts state funds will decrease, just as new requirements come into place. The costs of the Texas Educational Assessment of Minimum Skills (TEAMS) tests, the extension of the maximum class size to grades three and four beginning in 1988, the extension of the career ladder to levels III and IV in subsequent years, and the requirement of a summer preschool program beginning in the summer of 1985 are all examples of requirements that will begin to affect districts while state funding remains level (or even declines) for most districts.

The practice of requiring districts to provide services without specifically providing funding is common, but it leads to several problems.

One of them is local resistance to state mandates. Another is a pattern of inequality, since wealthy districts can fund additional requirements without any trouble, while poor districts must struggle to increase funds and must sometimes pay for new requirements from funds that would otherwise go for the normal costs of instruction. In general, then, the practice in House Bill 72 of imposing requirements on districts without providing funding may generate problems for school districts over the next several years.

Funding for Capital Expenditures

The requirement of a maximum class size in House Bill 72 illustrates another continuing problem of school finance in Texas: the funding of capital expenditures. Because of high growth rates, school debt in Texas is very high. According to the Texas Comptroller of Public Accounts, Texas public school systems in 1981-82 reported the highest amount of total debt outstanding among all states, just under $4.7 billion.[17] This was an increase of 5.1 percent from the previous year and represented 13 percent of total debt of all public school systems in the United States. By comparison, Texas has 7.8 percent of all classroom teachers, 7 percent of all districts and 7.6 percent of total enrollment in the United States. Outstanding debt per capita was $318.72 in Texas, which ranks third behind Alaska and Wyoming. Texas ranks first among the ten industrial and five regional states in outstanding debt per capita.[18]

Currently, there are no provisions for state aid to cover capital costs. The result is another form of the equalization problem: as table 10 illustrates, wealthy districts have much higher capital expenditures than poor districts, even though their tax rates for debt service are much lower. Both the maximum class size requirement and the prekindergarten requirement in House Bill 72 will affect poor districts more than wealthy districts by necessitating additional classrooms, compounding the inequities that now exist.

The only real solution to this problem is to provide state aid specifically for construction. Thirty-one states provide some form of state aid for construction: three assume all costs, eight assume some fraction of costs, twenty provide grants for capital outlays; and eight make loans to districts or subsidize interest costs. Only fifteen states including Texas provide no aid for capital costs. Given the requirements of House Bill 72 that affect construction and the wealth-based inequalities in capital outlays, the idea of state aid for construction merits more attention in the future.

Changes in House Bill 72 and the Continuing Problem of Equalization

Although House Bill 72 reduced the differences between rich and poor districts, large disparities remain. As table 9 illustrates, the differences in the operating expenditures per pupil between the richest and poorest districts are still substantial--almost $1,200 per pupil. The disparities between moderately wealthy and moderately poor districts are also serious, and differences in teacher salaries compound the problem.

Table 10
Debt Service and Capital Outlays by Wealth, 1983-84

Wealth per Pupil	Debt Service Expenditures per Pupil	Capital Outlay Expenditures per Pupil	Debt Service Tax Rate
$ 0- 57,800	$104	$214	.200
57,800-111,400	147	230	.160
111,400-155,500	192	314	.140
155,500-191,271	218	254	.118
191,271-245,000	295	340	.126
245,000-342,500	292	444	.095
342,500-407,800	275*	406**	.066***
Over $407,800	389	811	.060
Statewide Average	$238	$350	.119

*Without Houston $341
**Without Houston $569
***Without Houston .085

The equalizing mechanism of House Bill 72 will probably grow slightly stronger in 1985-86. The basic allotment increases in 1985-86 from $1,290 to $1,350, a change that will add a roughly equal amount of state aid per pupil in rich and poor districts. The mechanism that gives House Bill 72 its equalizing power--the calculation of a local share of foundation school program costs that is larger for wealthier districts--will become more equalizing as the local share increases from 30 percent of total costs in 1984-85 to 33.3 percent in 1985-86 and thereafter. (This same mechanism also affects the calculation of the experienced teacher allotment.)

However, there are minimal provisions for state aid under House Bill 72 to increase after 1985-86 (except as attendance grows). With continued inflation, districts will increasingly be forced to raise local revenues to cover the costs of schooling, and these local revenues will inevitably be larger in wealthier districts. On the whole, then, the equalizing effects of House Bill 72 will begin to grow weaker after 1985-86.

We conclude, therefore, that the issue of equalization will remain a persistent problem in Texas. Expenditure differences have not been eliminated, and they may start to grow wider as the equalizing power of House Bill 72 is diluted in the future. The only real solutions will be increases in state aid, together with revisions in the patterns of aid among districts. Until such reforms are again possible, it is crucial to continue monitoring the patterns of spending within Texas.

Appendix
A DESCRIPTION OF DATA SOURCES

In this chapter we relied on data from the Texas Education Agency and from a survey conducted by the Texas Association of School Boards and the Texas Association of School Administrators.

The TASB/TASA data were collected by a survey mailed to all districts in the fall of 1984. Usable responses were provided by 679 of the 1,068 districts in the state. While this sample is not complete, it appears to be biased only in underrepresenting small, wealthy districts. For the districts responding to the survey, 1983-84 ADA was 3,063, compared to 2,557 for all districts; property value per pupil was $344,829, compared to a statewide average of $394,707; and operating expenditures per pupil were $2,873, very close to the average of $2,923 for all districts. Because of the underrepresentation of wealthy districts in the TASB/TASA data, results based on these figures do not show as much variation as TEA data do. However, the patterns revealed by the two sources of data are identical. Table 2 in this appendix presents some comparisons of the TEA and the TASB/TASA data for expenditures and teacher salaries.

The TASB data included responses about budget figures, salaries, and additional costs due to the maximum class size and the career ladder. Personnel figures were broken down by category (administrators, teachers, auxiliary personnel, paraprofessionals, and others), as were payroll expenditures. Teacher salaries were reported by low, average, and high salaries. Additional costs included the number of additional classrooms and teachers needed and the number of existing but unused classrooms. Information was provided regarding the amount of career ladder supplement being paid, the number of teachers eligible for level II of the career ladder and the number of people actually being promoted, and the districts which also offer other merit pay incentives. In most cases, this information was gathered for 1983-84 and 1984-85, allowing a consistent comparison of changes.

The TEA data used were complete for all 1,068 districts. The 1983-84 data from TEA included total revenue figures from various sources, federal revenue by purpose, expenditure figures by purpose, personnel by category (e.g., support/administration, teachers, aides, and total personnel), total minimum and actual salary figures, enrollment figures by ethnic group, attendance, membership, and property value. For 1984-85, TEA provided us with the data used in the fall of 1984 for the preliminary calculation of state aid, in order to analyze the amounts of projected aid that districts had to rely on when planning their 1984-85 expenditures. These figures included information on the components of state aid, including the costs of special programs, calculation of foundation school program costs, experienced teacher allotments, equalization enrichment, equalization transition, and the PDI. While these are preliminary rather than final calculations of state aid, the differences between preliminary and final calculations depend in most cases on changes in ADA; therefore, the per pupil figure reported in this chapter should not be substantially affected.

Appendix table 1 presents correlation coefficients among wealth, size (ADA), percent black, percent Hispanic, and various measures of expenditures, salaries, and state aid. These correlations describe the basic relationships in the data available to us.

Another data source is a Fall 1984 survey sent by TEA to all school districts, asking questions similar to those on the TASB/TASA questionnaire about planned expenditures and salaries for 1983-84. While we planned to analyze these data as well, problems in transferring data between TEA and the LBJ School prevented us from doing so. A preliminary analysis of these data, performed by Lynn Moak of Lynn Moak Consulting Services, is available, however, and the TASB/TASA data and TEA's fall data are compared in Appendix table 2. While the numbers differ because the TEA sample includes more districts, the patterns are identical.

TEA divides districts into twenty Education Service Center (ESC) regions. In this study, the twenty regions were aggregated further into six, as follows:

1. Panhandle: regions 16 and 17

2. North Central Texas: regions 9, 10, and 11

3. West Texas: regions 18 and 19

4. South Texas: regions 1, 2, 3, and 20

5. Central Texas: regions 12, 13, 14, and 15

6. East Texas: regions 4, 5, 6, 7, and 8

Appendix Table 1
Correlation Coefficients

	Wealth per Pupil	ADA 83-84	Percent Black	Percent Hispanic
Wealth per Pupil	1.000	.161	.147	-.149
Total Expenditure per Pupil, 83-84	.495	-.020	-.001	-.218
Debt Service per Pupil, 83-84	.220	-.123	-.212	-.270
Capital Expenditures per Pupil, 83-84	.174	-.120	-.162	-.105
Operating Expenditures per Pupil, 83-84	.610	.100	.191	-.187
Operating Expenditures per Pupil, 84-85	.314	.030	.099	-.055
Change in Operating Expenditure	-.034	-.032	-.017	.065
Low Teacher Salary, 83-84	.434	.473	.335	-.264
Low Teacher Salary, 84-85	.376	.247	.198	-.165
Change in Low Teacher Salary	-.234	-.438	-.276	.181
Average Teacher Salary, 83-84	.383	.366	.310	-.305
Average Teacher Salary, 84-85	.335	.205	.190	-.256
Change in Average Teacher Salary	-.161	-.392	-.288	.090
High Teacher salary, 83-84	.301	.671	.509	-.086
High Teacher Salary, 84-85	.291	.622	.498	-.102
Change in High Teacher Salary	-.094	-.247	-.116	-.011
Price Differential Index	.204	.403	.268	-.110
Equalization Enrichment Aid	-.470	-.335	-.393	.436
Experienced Teacher Allotment	-.154	.322	.328	.801
Equalization Transition Entitlement	-.458	.128	-.177	-.176

Appendix Table 2
A Comparison of TASB/TASA and TEA Data

Wealth per Pupil	Expenditures per Student		Average Teacher Salary	
	1983-84	1984-85	1983-84	1984-85
TASB/TASA Data				
Under $96,587	$ 2,045	$ 2,457	$17,301	$20,436
$ 96,587-124,774	2,165	2,413	17,877	20,952
124,775-155,063	2,244	2,409	18,094	21,202
155,064-200,121	2,396	2,648	19,866	22,756
200,122-278,973	2,546	2,783	20,672	23,106
278,974-469,267	2,922	3,146	22,006	23,872
Over $469,267	3,793	3,986	22,025	24,623
TEA Data				
Under $96,587	$1,908	$2,478	$17,595	$20,856
$ 96,587-124,774	2,128	2,603	18,827	21,563
124,775-155,063	2,175	2,554	18,728	21,200
155,064-200,121	2,361	2,673	20,057	22,392
200,122-278,973	2,551	2,849	20,977	23,328
278,974-469,267	2,829	3,101	22,175	24,011
Over $469,267	4,122	4,551	22,201	24,743

Notes

[1]Based on TEA computer runs dated March 28, 1985.

[2]Stephen Carroll, The Search for Equity in School Finance: Summary and Conclusions, Report R-2420-NIE (Santa Monica: Rand, March 1979).

[3]The correlation with wealth is .204 and with size, .403. However, these relationships are not strictly linear, since the wealthiest and poorest districts have moderate values for the PDI. The component of the PDI based on the low-income students moderates the tendency for the PDI to be even more correlated with wealth.

[4]"Report of the Price Differential Index Advisory Committee to the Texas State Board of Education," Texas Education Agency, November 10, 1984.

[5]The calculation of the PDI is based on a three-step regression procedure with the log of teacher salary as the dependent variable. The three-step procedure itself is bizarre and biases the coefficients used in calculating the index. In addition, an endogenous variation (the district tax rate) is inappropriately included, and many variables are arbitrarily excluded. The director of this Policy Research Project, W. Norton Grubb, is currently working with Representative Paul Colbert to devise a price index that is theoretically and empirically more sound.

[6]That is, EEA is a matching grant, where the rate of matching is inversely related to property value per pupil, as in a district power equalizing or percentage equalizing formula. However, because the tax rate that is matched is subject to a maximum, the EEA formula becomes a nonmatching grant for districts whose tax rates are over a maximum.

[7]Between 1984-85 and 1985-86, the enrichment equalization allotment decreases by $24.6 million, or 4.9 percent. Personal communication, Madeleine McCulley, July 23, 1985.

[8]These figures are statewide averages or district averages weighted by the number of teachers. For unweighted averages, see table 7. The other data reported in this chapter are weighted by some measure of district size, either average daily attendance or numbers of teachers.

[9]Based on data collected by the American Compensation Association in its 1983 Salary Budget Survey.

[10]Data on teacher salaries in earlier years comes from the Texas Research League Analysis 5, no. 3, (March 1984), Table 5.

[11]The TASB/TASA survey asked districts to report their total teacher payroll, numbers of teachers, and average teacher salary; thus, there were two ways of calculating average teacher salary, giving slightly different results--$22,455 and $22,800 in 1984-85. TEA's estimate of average teacher salary for the state in 1984-85 is $22,648, right between these two estimates.

[12]The correlation is .131.

[13]The figures may not be perfectly comparable. The TASB/TASA survey asked for the 1984-85 operating budget and fall enrollment, and 1984-85 operating expenditure per pupil is the ratio of these two. The comparable 1983-84 figure based on TEA data is the operating expenditure divided by average daily membership. TEA's figure for operating expenditure per pupil in 1984-85 is $2,810, very close to the TASB/TASA figure of $2,827.

[14]These results are similar to findings in the San Antonio area, in Nicholas DeLuca, "An Investigation of the Initial Impact of House Bill 72 on the School Districts of Bexar County," Education Council of the Greater San Antonio Chamber of Commerce (February 1985).

[15]According to TEA's data from its Fall 1984 survey, state revenue increased from 51.4 percent of state-local revenue in 1983-84 to 52.6 percent in 1984-85.

[16]Joint Select Committee on Fiscal Policy, Funding Texas State Government: An Analysis of Taxes and Selected Non-Tax Revenue (Austin, January 1985), chapter 1.

[17]Comptroller of Public Accounts, Comptroller's Education Workpapers, vol. IV, Fiscal Issues (Austin, 1984).

[18]The ten industrial states are New Jersey, New York, Pennsylvania, Massachusetts, Illinois, Florida, Ohio, Michigan, California, and Texas. The five regional states are Oklahoma, Louisiana, Arkansas, New Mexico, and Texas.

CHAPTER TWO
REFORMS TO IMPROVE THE QUALITY OF TEACHERS

One of the most important areas of reform in House Bill 72 concerns the treatment of teachers. Several changes--including salary increases, the establishment of a career ladder, a required competency exam, and a state-funded college loan program for prospective teachers--were based on the philosophy that nothing can be done to improve the quality of education in Texas without changes in the teaching profession. The reforms were therefore designed to attract more people to teaching, to retain the best teachers, and to eliminate incompetent teachers.

These changes have been among the most controversial elements of House Bill 72. While teachers have acknowledged that there is room for improvement within their profession, they have remained ambivalent over the reforms and have questioned whether they were a means of enhancing teaching or an insult to teachers. Many administrators share the ambivalence of teachers; as a superintendent in a school district of moderate size and wealth stated, "The provisions of H.B. 72 are a slap in the face to the teachers. Teachers could have accepted the reforms more willingly if they hadn't been put down. The bill has had a demoralizing effect and will cause many teachers to leave the profession based on principle."[1] Of course, other teachers and administrators feel that the teacher-related reforms enacted in H.B. 72 will attract highly qualified individuals to the teaching profession and enhance the quality of teaching. However, the ambivalence of teachers toward House Bill 72 raises the possibility that these reforms will continue to be difficult to implement and contradictory in their effects, enhancing teaching on the one hand and degrading teachers on the other.

In this chapter we examine the first year's reactions to the teacher-related reforms in House Bill 72. For several of these reforms it is too early to judge the effects of the legislation, although it is possible to describe the reactions of administrators and teachers. Above all, the teacher-related reforms of House Bill 72 raise questions about their effectiveness in improving the quality of teachers--questions that remain crucial despite our inability to answer them definitively.

TEACHER SALARIES AND INCREASES IN HOUSE BILL 72

The fact that public school teachers are underpaid has been a universal criticism, from both inside and outside the teaching profession. Higher salaries are generally considered to be a way of attracting highly qualified individuals into teaching and retaining good teachers. As a result, a teacher pay raise was brought up in several legislative sessions before the 1983 session. Prior to the passage of House Bill 72, salary increases were the principal concern of teacher organizations,[2] and the promise of a teacher pay raise was an excellent way for 1982 gubernatorial candidate Mark White to win the support of teachers.

Since the support of teacher organizations was the prime factor in his victory, Governor White made teacher salary increases a top priority in the 1983 legislative session. However, because of declining state revenues, the legislature did not pass a school finance bill permitting salary increases from state funds.

Because of the political difficulties of increasing taxes in Texas, the legislature would consider a tax increase for teacher pay raises only with the most thorough justification. The Select Committee on Public Education was the mechanism established by the legislature to examine teacher pay, as well as to recommend solutions for the problem of equalization. The committee recommended both an across-the-board pay raise and a merit pay plan, or career ladder, intended to encourage higher standards in the teaching profession by rewarding excellent teachers. However, the Select Committee would not endorse a salary increase and career ladder without a competency exam for teachers, because of a perception that incompetent teachers were too numerous and would otherwise continue to undermine the quality of teaching. The SCOPE recommendations, tying salary increases to a career ladder and a competency exam, were enacted by the legislature, joining these controversial provisions to the more widely accepted increases in state funds to boost teacher salaries.

Prior to House Bill 72, the Texas public education compensation plan consisted of eighteen pay grades and included teachers and administrators as well as support staff like aides, clerical workers, custodians, and cafeteria workers. Monthly minimum salaries ranged from $558 for an educational aide with no experience to $4,052 for a superintendent in a large district with over fourteen years of experience. In effect, the state set a minimum salary level for all public school employees. The total amount of state funds for salaries allocated to each district was determined by using personnel unit values. An educational aide, for example, was worth .55 personnel unit (PU); a teacher was worth 1.00 PU, and a large district superintendent's salary was worth 2.50 PUs. Because state funding was tied so closely to the numbers of local personnel, the structure of local salaries tended to follow the structure of the state's pay grades. Furthermore, teachers tended to view salary increases as state decisions rather than local district decisions. In effect, the structure of state aid limited, in practice if not in law, the ability of districts to set their own salary policies.

House Bill 72 abandoned the close link between state aid and school district personnel. Under the new funding formula, a district's funding for salaries is included in its total state aid, which in turn is based on the number of pupils rather than the number of personnel units. House Bill 72 also included a new set of minimum monthly salaries applicable to teachers, counselors, and administrators (but not support staff) ranging from $1,520 per month for those with no experience to $2,660 for those with ten or more years of experience. The new minimum salary for a teacher with a bachelor's degree was an increase of 37 percent over the 1983-84 minimum of $1,111 per month.

In several ways, then, House Bill 72 provides substantially greater freedom to local districts in setting salaries. Rather than being tied to an elaborate minimum salary structure, with different pay grades for types of employees, experience, and degrees, districts are now free to adopt their own salary structures. No longer are increases in state funds tied directly to personnel, and it has become clear that districts are free to spend state funds as they wish as long as teachers and administrators are paid at least the state minimum salary levels. Similarly, it has become clear that salary increases are now a local decision.

A common misconception which occurred after the enactment of House Bill 72 was the idea that all teachers were to get a pay raise of at least $170 a month, an amount which roughly equaled the increase in state aid divided by the number of teachers. In fact, as the data in the previous chapter illustrate, there were substantial variations among districts in pay increases in the first year of House Bill 72, with poor districts increasing salaries more than wealthy districts, and some districts failing to increase salaries at all.

As we have seen in chapter 1, the purpose of increasing teacher salaries was in fact fulfilled. Average teacher salaries in 1984-85 increased by an average of nearly 10 percent, substantially higher than the rate of inflation of about 3.5 percent and higher than the estimated growth rate of salaries in private employment of about 6.6 percent. However, these average salary increases were not evenly spread among teachers. The largest pay increases, averaging 22 percent, went to beginning teachers, while the highest teacher salaries increased by only 8.5 percent. As a result, salary differentials between experienced and inexperienced teachers have been substantially compressed in the first year of House Bill 72.

One justification for increasing the salaries of beginning teachers disproportionately is to attract more qualified individuals into the teaching profession, and some observers are optimistic that House Bill 72 will improve teacher quality in this way. However, to the extent that teachers are motivated by salaries, the compression of salary differentials will reduce the incentive to remain in teaching. In our interviews, experienced teachers expressed frustration and resentment over the fact that they were not earning much more than their inexperienced counterparts.

Being a dedicated teacher with 8 1/2 years experience and 21 hours towards a master's degree (not to mention a single parent), I am deeply chagrined to see my first pay check reflect a raise of only $51.07. I feel especially tormented each time I read an article in the newspaper or a magazine, or hear an announcement on the TV or radio "news" mentioning teachers' tremendous pay raise this year.[3]

The greatest concern was voiced by teachers whose income from teaching was their family's sole source of support; for them, local salary increases did not come close to providing a comfortable living, except for those employed in wealthy districts where the cost of living was low. In general, few experienced teachers felt that the recent pay raise was sufficient, and many of them felt that the salary changes induced by House Bill 72 were yet another insult to teachers.

The reaction of experienced teachers to the first year of House Bill 72 suggests that the problem of teacher salaries is not fully resolved. This is especially the case because in the next few years there will be no real increases in state aid to districts, in contrast to the 20 percent increase in 1984-85; therefore, salary increases will have to come out of local revenues. One question this raises is whether experienced teachers are likely to leave the profession because of low salary differentials. The teachers we interviewed reported that they are unlikely to leave despite their perceptions of low salaries, because most of them rank other factors--especially the joys and challenges of teaching--as more important than pay.[4] Nevertheless, the changes in House Bill 72 implicitly assume that teachers do respond to pay differences; therefore, the long-run effects of compressing salaries on experienced teachers should remain a concern.

MERIT PAY AND THE TEXAS CAREER LADDER

Although the career ladder adopted in House Bill 72 was a substantial departure from previous practice, merit pay for teachers was not a new issue to Texas or the nation. Merit pay plans have been attempted (and have failed) since the 1920s, usually coinciding with conservative political trends and movements for educational "excellence."

A form of merit pay was the dominant method used to compensate teachers in the early part of the twentieth century and was prevalent in the 1920s. Single salary schedules, which based teacher pay on years of experience and education, were adopted in the 1930s and 1940s in a move to give equal pay to teachers with similar experience and training. Merit pay reemerged in the late 1950s and early 1960s in response to the demand for improved educational quality stimulated by the Sputnik "crisis." However, many of the merit pay plans established then were short-lived; most of them foundered because of continuing problems in judging merit and the continued antipathy of teachers.[5]

During the 1980s, merit pay was "rediscovered" as an educational reform, as part of a more conservative political climate and a renewed emphasis on educational excellence. The report of several national commissions, including A Nation at Risk: The Imperative for Educational Reform, endorsed some form of merit pay plan, and President Reagan supported merit pay in his 1984 campaign. Supporters asserted that merit-based salary schedules would enhance respect for the teaching profession by providing greater incentives for excellent teaching.[6]

But fiscal restrictions at both the federal and state levels also influenced the movement to increase salaries of the most competent teachers only. Ronald Reagan, in a commencement address at Seton Hall University in

1983, stated, "Teachers should be paid and promoted on the basis of their merit and competence. Hard-earned tax dollars should encourage the best. They have no business rewarding incompetence and mediocrity."[7]

Carl D. Perkins, chair of the House Committee on Education and Labor, responded to President Reagan's idea of merit pay by appointing a Merit Pay Task Force to analyze the issue. The committee's report, published in 1983, focused on the lack of respect given to the teaching profession, based on a comparison of its required training and salaries with other professions. The task force recommended that higher pay be accompanied by higher state standards for teachers and recommended experiments with performance-based pay like those being considered in Tennessee, California, and Florida--three states which had proposed programs to recognize outstanding teachers in the fall of 1982.[8] As a result of all this national attention, merit pay and career ladder plans became the focus of attention in state legislatures, state boards, and departments of education during 1983. Thus, the recommendation of a career ladder by SCOPE and its adoption by the Texas legislature in the summer of 1984 developed not only from statewide concerns with the quality of instruction, but also from national interest in merit pay.[9]

The Structure of the Career Ladder in Texas
The career ladder established by House Bill 72 consists of four levels, with all teachers and administrators who have completed a probationary year starting at level I, and progressing up the ladder based on criteria that include classroom performance, degrees achieved and other forms of coursework, and experience. House Bill 72 specified that promotion to levels III and IV would be postponed until 1987 and 1989 so that only level II was relevant in 1984-85.

The criteria for promotion to levels II, III, and IV include degrees, coursework, and experience. The requirements are complex and permit trade-offs; they are fully described in an appendix to this chapter. For example, promotion to level II requires either a bachelor's degree, three years' experience, and 9 semester hours beyond the bachelor's degree or 135 hours of advanced academic coursework; or a master's degree and two years of teaching experience. The requirements for levels III and IV similarly permit trade-offs between degrees and other coursework and experience. Because promotion up the career ladder requires additional education at every stage, the career ladder provides some incentive for teachers to continue their education, either in coursework based in colleges and universities or in other advanced academic training programs. In our interviews, we found that districts are generally encouraging the advancement of teachers up the career ladder by providing additional training through in-service programs or by contracting with local colleges and universities to provide courses that would comply with the state requirements. Often, these arrangements are established to minimize the burden on teachers; for example, Clint, Socorro, San Elizario, and Fabens ISDs have all contracted with the University of Texas at El Paso to provide courses located within the school districts so that teachers do not have to drive to El Paso after a day's teaching.

However, the most controversial requirements of the career ladder are those related to performance, rather than to degrees and experience levels. House Bill 72 established an appraisal process to evaluate the performance of teachers and administrators, with five performance categories: unsatisfactory; below expectations; satisfactory; exceeding expectations; and clearly outstanding. While House Bill 72 gives the State Board of Education considerable discretion in establishing an appraisal process, no decisions on this process were made by the board during the 1984-85 school year. Therefore, districts had considerable freedom to develop their own methods of evaluating teachers, with few guidelines and little advice from the state about how to develop an effective assessment mechanism.

In this vacuum, the Texas Association of School Boards and the Texas Association of School Administrators recommended the following guidelines for districts to consider prior to selecting level II teachers.[10] First, a list of teachers who met the minimum state requirements for level II should be compiled early. This would give the district ample time to decide how many teachers qualified and how many would be chosen, based on funding decisions. The administrative members of the selection committee should then be appointed. According to House Bill 72, the committee must include a principal, an administrator responsible for personnel, and another administrator. Multiple committees were, of course, necessary in larger districts. The committee was required to appoint two teachers to level II, who would also serve on the committee. Once the committee was established, it should plan the selection process and determine stricter local criteria (if necessary). The TASB and TASA recommended that local committees consider the following:

1. To what extent can and should stricter performance criteria be established?

2. How far back should performance evaluations be considered?

3. Should all professional training hours be considered of equal value?

4. Should teachers who are newly transferred to the districts be considered eligible?

5. What will be the time schedule and responsibilities of committee members?

The committee could then decide whether to announce its decision for level II promotions publicly. Decisions would be final and could not be appealed. Finally, the full supplement should be paid prior to the end of the 1984-85 contract period. It could be disbursed in a lump sum or in divided payments.

In general, the novelty of the career ladder and uncertainty about procedures--including uncertainty about what rules the State Board would promulgate--generated considerable uncertainty about how to proceed and led not only to differences in the way districts evaluated performance but also to varied implementation schedules. In general, the implementation of the career ladder seemed to depend on the organizational ability of the district's superintendent or personnel director. Some districts completed their career ladder evaluations in the fall of 1984. Others waited until the end of the school year, admitting that they hoped to learn from the successes and mistakes of others. One superintendent in a small district stated, for example, that he would not begin implementing the career ladder until Dallas had approved a career ladder plan. This wait-and-see attitude appeared to be limited to smaller districts; however, there were exceptions. By late January, El Paso ISD had not begun implementing the career ladder either.

Some smaller districts had, however, proceeded with career ladder implementation based on their own needs. For example, Allen ISD, established stricter performance criteria than House Bill 72 required, in the event that more teachers were identified as eligible than could be supported.[11]

Other districts had adopted methods already being used for the career ladder. For example, Taylor had had its own career ladder program for the previous three to four years, advancing teachers based on its own criteria; principals were primarily responsible for evaluating all eligible teachers. The district decided to use its own procedures for evaluating teachers under House Bill 72.

Regardless of the evaluation procedures used, teachers feared that personnel politics would be an inevitable result of the career ladder. A number of teachers voiced concern that personalities, favoritism, and nepotism would influence career ladder decisions. In some small school districts, teachers claimed that every teacher was related to or personally knew at least one member of the career ladder committee and expressed concern over the potential animosity in small districts where everyone knows everyone else. Some teachers anticipated not only resentment against principals and other evaluators but against each other and feared that a competitive atmosphere would be generated.

Another source of resentment among teachers has come from a difference of opinion on how the career ladder should work. House Bill 72 permits districts substantial discretion in setting the procedures for promotion on the career ladder, so that a district can set criteria which are relatively loose or relatively stringent. This means that, of teachers eligible for promotion (with the required combination of degrees, coursework, and experience), a district can promote all or only some of them. This allows districts discretion not only to establish their own criteria for promotion, but also to adjust the level of expenditures on the career ladder, since promoting a larger fraction of eligible teachers requires greater expenditures. However, many teachers and teacher groups are disappointed that less than 100 percent of eligible teachers are being promoted. In effect, many teachers have argued that the state ought to impose minimum standards for promotion that all districts must respect, rather than allowing for local discretion.

The preliminary information cited in the previous chapter suggests that districts have in fact exercised a great deal of discretion in their promotion practices. Of the 679 districts responding to questionnaires administered by TASB and TASA in the fall of 1984, only one-third responded to questions about the career ladder; the remainder reported that they had not yet made any decisions and were waiting for guidelines from the State Board of Education. (This low response rate corroborates the uncertainty and confusion about the career ladder which we discovered in interviews.) The districts which responded reported that 56 percent of teachers would be eligible for level II of the career ladder in 1984-85; of those eligible, districts planned to promote 71 percent; that overall almost 34 percent of teachers would be promoted to level II. However, these averages may be misleading because of large variations among districts. For example, 13 percent of districts responded that they would promote one-third or less of eligible teachers to level II, while 29 percent reported that they would promote all eligible teachers. While these results are not conclusive because of the limited responses to the TASB/TASA survey, they are suggestive of the direction that the career ladder might take.

The Funding of the Career Ladder

House Bill 72 presumes that districts will provide a salary supplement of $2,000 to every teacher promoted on the career ladder, unless the state allotments to fund the career ladder are insufficient; then the supplements can be reduced to $1,500. The intention in House Bill 72 is that the career ladder be funded from state rather than local revenues. For 1984-95, $100 per pupil was allocated to every district for an Educational Improvement and Career Ladder Allotment. Districts were required to spend $30 of this amount on career ladder supplements, with $35 per pupil to be spent on salaries for personnel other than classroom teachers, and $35 per pupil for any other legal purpose (including further career ladder supplements). In effect, then, this allotment amounted to a grant of $30 per pupil for the career ladder, and a flat grant of $70 per pupil which districts could use in other ways. In our interviews, it appears that the majority of school districts are using exactly $30 per pupil to fund career ladder supplements, although there are some exceptions. Thus, most districts appear to be proceeding cautiously with the career ladder in spending the minimum amount required, rather than spending more than $30 per pupil to promote a larger fraction of teachers or to pay them a higher supplement. Such caution may be justifiable, because promotion on the career ladder has future as well as current consequences for salary costs: teachers promoted to level II continue receiving salary supplements at that level (unless their performance falls "below expectations"), and they are also eligible for subsequent promotion to level III with additional salary supplements.

Of the districts that responded to the TASB/TASA questionnaire, 59 percent planned to provide a supplement of $1,500 in 1984-85, while only 28 percent planned to give the full $2,000 supplement; the remaining districts planned to give a supplement between $1,500 and $2,000. Based on this information, it appears that the amount of state aid allocated for the career ladder supplement is insufficient in most districts to fund the $2,000 supplement that House Bill 72 presumes. In this sense, the charge--primarily from teacher groups--that the career ladder has not been fully funded is valid. But from the viewpoint of district administrators, caution in setting these supplements may be appropriate, because of uncertainty about the numbers of teachers promoted and the size of future state appropriations for the career ladder.

The funding of the career ladder presents another way in which wealth differentials could affect practices among districts. Because wealthy districts can spend more on the career ladder--either from funds allocated through the Educational Improvement and Career Ladder Allotment or from their own revenues--it is possible that wealthy districts will promote a higher fraction of teachers up the career ladder and pay them higher supplements, compared to property-poor districts. In the preliminary data available from TASB/TASA, we found no indication that wealth differences affected the initial implementation of the career ladder. However, the possibility of such a pattern merits future monitoring, since--if the salary incentives of the career ladder work as intended--low funding of the career ladder in poor districts would cause the most able teachers to leave for wealthier districts where their talents would more likely to be rewarded.

Evaluating the Career Ladder

It is difficult to evaluate objectively the attributes of the career ladder in Texas based on national studies in favor of merit pay. The congressional Merit Pay Task Force argued in favor of merit pay as a means of affording teachers greater respect. A Nation at Risk and the report of the Twentieth Century Fund Task Force on Federal Elementary and Secondary Education Policy reiterated the argument,[12] but without evidence about what the effects of merit pay would be.

Other general arguments in favor of merit pay can only be substantiated on a subjective level. Susan Moore Johnson, in a report on the pros and cons of merit pay, elaborated some traditional arguments:

1. Merit pay is consistent with free enterprise.

2. Merit pay would keep better teachers in education while dissuading ineffective teachers from remaining in the profession.

3. Merit pay would stimulate teachers to be critical of their work and promote healthy competition.

4. Taxpayers would be more willing to support public education if teachers were paid based on performance.[13]

The only general argument listed above that can be closely substantiated as an objective rationale for implementing merit pay in Texas is the last. Public opinion polls have indicated that taxpayers are in favor of merit pay as a means of supporting good teachers.[14] The other arguments are no more than subjective opinions. There is some evidence that higher salaries do have an effect in preventing teachers from leaving the profession, or leaving for other districts;[15] however, these results do not indicate whether the teachers who are most responsive to salary differences are the most able or the most incompetent.

There is no doubt that outstanding and productive teachers should be recognized and that the public should "get what it pays for." Unfortunately, traditional measures of evaluating productivity which are used in business, for example, can not be applied in measuring output in education. It seems unlikely that a uniform appraisal system for teachers can be developed in Texas or the rest of the country. Most important, what has been shown is that teachers who are under some form of performance-based evaluation would spend time with the most capable children as a way of appearing to produce the greatest "output."[16]

The evaluation appraisal system in Texas, as mandated in House Bill 72, is an example of the problems which can occur in performance-based evaluations. Because of the lack of a uniform, statewide appraisal mechanism, a staff member of the Texas Senate Education Committee stated, "We're operating on an indefinite and legally weak appraisal system."[17]

The history of merit pay is not full of successes either. A 1978 Educational Research Study found that one half of the reported merit pay plans studied had been in effect for less than five years. The reasons for the past failures of merit pay plans included administrative problems, personnel and collective bargaining controversies, and poor financial conditions. More to the point, teacher performance did not appear to improve as a result of the merit pay plans which were evaluated.[18] The districts where merit pay plans are successful seem to have several characteristics in common: they generally have relatively high salary schedules, good working conditions, a history of amicable relations between teachers and administrators, voluntary merit pay plans, an absence of quotas on the numbers of teachers who can be promoted, and extensive teacher representation in the design of the plan.[19] While these conditions can be met in some Texas districts, they are likely to fail in a substantial number if only because the career ladder is not funded generously enough to eliminate quotas and because, realistically, not all districts can have the exemplary salaries and working conditions that have helped merit pay plans thrive.

Despite the problems inherent in merit pay, the career ladder has been enacted; the task at hand is to implement the career ladder so that it has the greatest chance for improving the quality of teaching. There is a need for a uniform appraisal system to be developed, especially one that draws on the successful experiences with merit pay systems in other states. Some balance between uniformity and local discretion will have to be established, given the diversity of districts within Texas. But the most important task will be to monitor the effectiveness of the career ladder, motivating teachers and preventing good teachers from leaving the profession, since there is no educational justification for a merit pay plan that fails to improve the quality of teaching.

COMPETENCY TESTING

The Select Committee on Public Education recommended that a competency exam be administered to all teachers currently in the profession. In fact, SCOPE would not endorse any aspect of the education reform package if the competency exam provision were not included. Partly because of the intense lobbying of H. Ross Perot, the head of SCOPE, the legislature adopted this controversial provision, to be implemented in the 1985-86 school year. The provision of the competency exam was, in a sense, an extension of Senate Bill 50 (legislated in 1981), which requires that students take a state-normed basic skills test prior to enrolling in teacher education programs. (This test, designed to eliminate low achievers prior to their entering teaching, was first administered in 1984.)

House Bill 72 required that all teachers pass an exam proving their ability to read and write, their knowledge of the subject matter they are teaching, and their ability to perform the job. The law provided that the test must be passed by the 1985-86 school year. The type of exam was not specified, but was left to the State Board of Education. Teachers and administrators were concerned, because the scope of the exam was unknown. Teachers were also insulted, because they felt their profession was once again being assaulted by a group of individuals who had little or no experience in teaching. An element of fear has also been an issue: many teachers are afraid of the competency test even though they feel that they are competent. Many have not been students for quite some time and fear that they will be tested on subject matter with which they are unfamiliar.

The intrinsic problems with competency testing must also be considered. It was almost universally agreed, among both the administrators and the teachers we interviewed, that performance on standardized exams has little relationship to an individual's teaching ability. In fact, a number of administrators said that they knew very bright individuals who would have no trouble passing conventional exams, yet were poor instructors. As Dr. Thomas Murphy, a principal in Weslaco, stated, "Knowledge of Horace Mann does not ensure competency. The exam should focus on what teachers know about kids and learning."[20] Conversely, many administrators and teachers felt that some excellent classroom teachers might fail a competency exam that did not adequately consider teaching skills; many felt that any written competency tests should be supplemented by evaluations of classroom performance.

Still another practical difficulty that arose was the apparent need to devise a variety of tests for all the different subject areas taught in the public schools. Districts were also concerned about the costs of testing, and whether these costs would have to be borne by the districts themselves or by the state.

However, the State Board clarified many anxieties on the test when it decided that teachers would be required to take only a basic skills test. Beyond that, subject matter tests would be required for individuals who have experienced difficulties on the basic skills test. However, other problems have not yet been resolved. One of these is the cost of testing. Another is the question of what happens to those teachers who fail the basic skills test. Some administrators feel that shortages of teachers will be exacerbated, either because some teachers fail the basic skills tests or because some leave teaching rather than take the test. Others, especially those in districts with large numbers of black and Hispanic teachers, fear that a larger proportion of minority teachers will fail the exam, based on experiences elsewhere with competency exams.

It is difficult to weigh the value of competency exams, since there has been so little experience with this method of improving teaching. There is a real need to improve the quality of teaching. However, some of the arguments against an exam as a way of doing this seem correct--especially the view that incompetence in classroom teaching cannot be detected through a standardized exam. In other states that have enacted competency exams, there has in fact been a marked tendency for minority teachers to fail tests more than white teachers. Such tests have therefore exacerbated shortages of minority teachers, of bilingual teachers, and of teachers for inner-city and rural schools--at a time when teacher shortages are growing worse.[21] In general, tests to eliminate weak teachers rather than policies to enhance the ability of prospective teachers have a negative and punitive aspect which teachers resent. As a result, the competency exam provides another example of the contradictory effects of House Bill 72, which simultaneously enhances the status and pay of teachers in some ways and degrades them in others.

The real question is whether a competency exam is an effective way to improve the quality of teaching, given the other mechanisms available. Many teachers and administrators in Texas have suggested that greater emphasis be placed on improving teacher education and standards among new teachers; continuing education--including the kind of coursework necessary for advancement up the career ladder--is another mechanism for improvement. Since the competency exam has been enacted, the task remaining is to monitor the exam in 1985-86, to see what its effects are on different teachers and whether it eliminates those teachers judged ineffective by other criteria, and then to weigh whether a competency exam should continue to play a role among the variety of methods to improve teaching.

THE TEACHER LOAN PROGRAM

House Bill 72 also enacted a loan program for prospective teachers, to encourage outstanding high school students to enter the teaching profession. The loan program was in fact the only attempt in House Bill 72, apart from aid to increase teacher salaries, to deal with the fundamental problem that fewer able students are going into teaching. Unfortunately, the implementation of the loan program was marred by confusion and uncertainty. During the 1984 special session, the legislature appropriated $2.2 million in earned federal funds to support the program; however, the Attorney General initially ruled that the use of those funds was unconstitutional. To correct the problem, the 1985 legislature passed S.B. 1342, clarifying that federal funds are to be used to administer the loan program. Once the bill was signed in June 1985, the Coordinating Board began processing applications for the $481,000 available.

While most administrators and teachers agree that the loan is a positive step toward improving teacher quality, no one expects its effects to be substantial. Most observers predict that it will serve only a few students, most of whom would probably have entered the teaching field in any case. Future studies of the program should examine whether it encourages students of higher academic caliber to take advantage of the program; if so, expansion of the program should be considered.

CONCLUSIONS AND RECOMMENDATIONS

The teacher-related provisions of House Bill 72 are clearly sincere efforts to improve the quality of teaching. However, they have had several contradictory effects in the first year. Teacher salaries have gone up substantially on the average, but experienced teachers have seen their salaries go up much less than the salaries of inexperienced teachers, and some feel that their years of dedication are not being adequately recognized. Teachers have unanimously welcomed the recognition that they have been underpaid, but many have felt insulted by the career ladder and the competency exam legislated in House Bill 72. Since reforms of the teaching profession cannot possibly work without the cooperation of teachers, these feelings among teachers should be seriously considered, rather than being dismissed as peevish complaints.

But since House Bill 72 is law, the task at hand is to implement these provisions so as to maximize their potential for good and to monitor their effects. The early implementation of the career ladder by the state was not especially exemplary, particularly since the requirement was controversial and mechanisms for assessing classroom performance were rare. The state can do more, through either the Texas Education Agency or the regional Educational Service Centers, to determine what models of assessment have worked best and to circulate information about how to adapt such models to local conditions. With the State Board of Education now in full operation, the uncertainties which plagued districts in 1984-85 should abate, and the State Board should make sure that its subsequent rulings address the fears and uncertainties that local administrators and teachers feel. Similarly, the first year's administration of the basic skills test for teachers needs to be as supportive of teachers as possible, especially by giving them advanced information about the kind of test that will be administered, the standards necessary for passing, and the consequences of not passing.

Above all, the teacher-related provisions of House Bill 72 should be monitored to see if they work as intended. The good intentions behind these measures are not sufficient to ensure that they will in fact improve the quality of teaching. The abandonment of most merit pay plans developed in prior periods is one kind of evidence that this approach may generate more problems than it resolves. Information about local practices in promoting teachers up the career ladder, the changing attitudes of teachers and administrators as the career ladder and competency exams develop, the practices of rich and poor districts in funding the career ladder, and the numbers and kinds of teachers who fail the competency exam will all be guides for future policymaking. Above all, the state should make an effort to evaluate the effects of House Bill 72 on the quality of teaching, rather than leaving this central question to be answered by anecdote, ideology, or hyperbole, as is so often the case.

Several problems addressed by House Bill 72 are unlikely to disappear, however. Although state aid increased markedly in 1984-85 and facilitated teacher salary increases, such changes will not continue to occur, because aid to districts will level out in 1985-86 and 1986-87. Over the longer run, state revenues are likely to continue growing slowly, so that state aid increases will be possible only if the state's tax structure is revised. The problems of inadequate teacher salaries will continue to trouble the state. In addition, the basic issue of inadequate numbers of people going into teaching has been addressed only indirectly by House Bill 72, and the underlying causes--the low status of teaching, the opening of other professions to women, and the long-term deterioration of teacher salaries--are likely to continue.

A basic problem with salary increases, the career ladder, and the teacher loan program is that they assume that individuals respond to economic incentives in deciding whether to go into teaching or some other field. The evidence suggests instead that most current and prospective teachers are motivated not principally by money, but instead by love of teaching, concern for children, desire for professional autonomy, and the support of peers.

One goal of future policymaking in Texas might therefore be to investigate ways of enhancing these conditions, to complement the economic measures in House Bill 72 and to prevent the deterioration of teaching conditions that can be the result of criticism and of reform itself.

Appendix 1

CAREER LADDER LEVELS
BASED ON HOUSE BILL 72

I. Level I

   A. Requirements for a Level I Certificate
       --Completion of a probationary year of teaching

   B. Performance Standards for Level I
       --At least "satisfactory" performance during either
         of first two years in Level I

   C. Maintenance of Level I Certificate
       --Shall be valid for 3 full years
       --May be renewed once upon recommendation of the school
         district and the completion of 6 semester hours or
         90 hours of advanced academic training in an approved
         program in the area of certification or teaching assignment

II. Level II

   A. Requirements for a Level II Certificate
       --Possession of a valid Level I certificate
       --Bachelor's degree, 3 years' teaching experience,
         and 9 semester hours of higher education course work,
         or 135 hours of advanced academic training, or equivalent
         combination so that 1 semester hour of higher education
         work is equivalent to 15 hours of advanced academic
         training; or
       --Master's degree in subject taught, and two years of teaching
         experience
       --Recommendation by current or last employing school district

   B. Performance Standards for Level II
       --At least performance "exceeding expectations" during
         preceding year and "satisfactory" performance the other
         years

   C. Maintenance of Level II Certificate
       --Shall be valid for 5 years from the date of recommendation
         by the school district
       --Performance better than "below expectations"
       --May be renewable

III. Level III

A. Requirements for Level III Certificate
--Possession of a valid Level II certificate
--Bachelor's degree, and 8 years of teaching experience; or
--Master's degree and 5 years of teaching experience; or
--Doctorate and 3 years of teaching experience
--Recommendation by current or last employing school district

B. Performance Standards for Level III
--At least performance "exceeding expectations" during 3 of
   the preceding 4 years and at least "satisfactory"
   performance during the other year

C. Maintenance of Level III Certificate
--Shall be valid for five years from the date of
   recommendation by a school district; and
--Teacher shall be reassigned to Level II if satisfactory
   performance is not achieved for 2 consecutive years; or
--Reassigned to Level I if performance "below expectations"

IV. Level IV

A. Requirements for Level IV (Master Teacher) Certificate
--Possession of a valid Level III certificate
--Bachelor's degree and 11 years of teaching experience; or
--Master's degree and 8 years of teaching experience; or
--Doctorate and 5 years of teaching experience
--Recommendation by current or last employing school

B. Performance Standards for Level IV
--A school district may recommend a teacher for Level IV if
   certificate requirements are satisfied and the teacher is
   evaluated as "satisfactory," "exceeding expectations," or
   "clearly outstanding"

C. Level IV Maintenance
--"Clearly outstanding" performance during 2 of every 3 years
   and at least "satisfactory" performance the other year
--Teaching in classroom for not less than 60 percent of
   the school day
--Performance of 2 master teacher duties every 3 years
--3 semester hours of higher education course work, or
   45 hours of advanced academic training or an equivalent
   combination so that 1 semester hour of higher education
   work is equivalent to 15 hours of advanced academic
   training; or
--"Clearly outstanding" performance each year
--Teaching in classroom for not less than 60 percent of
   the school day
--Performance of 2 master duties every 3 years (master duties
   include supervising student teachers, assignment as a
   mentor, team leader, chairing a department, conducting
   advanced academic training, and assessing master teacher
   candidates)

Appendix 2

Tennessee

Governor Lamar Alexander of Tennessee argued in an address to the Education Forum on Career Ladders "that pay without respect won't attract and keep the best men and women in the classroom over the next several years . . . if we really want to keep and attract superior teachers, we had better think of some new and better ways to honor, respect, and award prestige to teachers."[22]

The merit pay (master teacher program) plan proposed in Tennessee was the means by which Governor Alexander hoped to afford teachers more respect. The plan was centralized and focused on rewarding performance; however, it also required advanced academic hours for promotion. The program established four levels: apprentice teacher, professional teacher, senior teacher, and master teacher. Teachers could apply for placement on any level and could be moved down the ladder in exchange for decreased responsibilities and salary. The Tennessee plan was centralized and based on statewide criteria which were implemented through a uniform, statewide assessment instrument.

Florida

In a special session of the Florida legislature, held in July 1983, a merit compensation program was passed. The program was designed to improve the public school program by providing incentives "to attract and retain qualified instructional personnel."[23] Like the Tennessee plan, the Florida program was centralized, and teacher evaluations were done through statewide written tests. Promotion in the plan, however, was based solely on the test and classroom performance and did not account for advanced academic training.

California

California's mentor teacher program was first implemented in 1983-84. The program was designed to encourage teachers to continue to pursue excellence, while providing outstanding teachers with incentives to remain in the profession. Teachers had to be nominated in order to apply for mentor teacher positions and were required to meet subjective minimum requirements, including substantial recent experience with classroom instruction and demonstration of exemplary teaching ability, as indicated by effective communication skills, subject matter knowledge, and mastery of a range of teaching strategies necessary to meet the needs of pupils in different contexts.[24]

Notes

[1]Interview with Forrest E. Watson, Superintendent of Schools, Hurst-Euless-Bedford ISD, Bedford, Texas, January 25, 1985.

[2]Interview with Representative Bill Haley, Texas State Legislature, Austin, Texas, February 12, 1985.

[3]Cynthia Walraven, "Teacher Chagrined, Tormented by Pay Raise, Tutorial Requirement," ATPE News 5, no. 3 (November/December 1984), 22.

[4]Of course, there is a selection mechanism at work: those individuals who do care more about salary may leave teaching, so that experienced teachers tend to be individuals who care more about their work and working conditions than about pay.

[5]Donna Blevins, "Merit Pay Overview" (paper presented to the National PTA Educational Commission and Teacher Issues Subcommittee, Chicago, Ill., January 13, 1984).

[6]Educational Research Service, Merit Pay Plans for Teachers: Status and Descriptions (Arlington, Va., 1983), 3.

[7]Ibid.

[8]U.S. Congress, House Committee on Education and Labor, Merit Pay Task Force Report, 98th Cong., 1st sess., October 1983.

[9]SCOPE was not the only group to design a career ladder. Three other proposals were developed by Representative Bill Haley and Senator Carl Parker, chairs of the House and Senate education committees, and by Representative Bill Hammond.

[10]Texas Association of School Boards and Texas Association of School Administrators, Implementing the Teacher Career Ladder (Austin, Texas, January 1985), 8.

[11]Ibid., 25.

[12]Making the Grade: Report of the Twentieth Century Fund Task Force on Federal Elementary and Secondary Education Policy (New York: Twentieth Century Fund, 1983).

[13]Susan Moore Johnson, Pros and Cons of Merit Pay (Bloomington, Ind.: Phi Delta Kappan Educational Foundation, 1984), 24.

[14]A Newsweek poll indicated that 80 percent of those questioned favored merit pay. Lu Van Loozen, "Some Points to Consider When You Discuss Merit Pay," American Association of School Administrators, Arlington, Va., 1983.

[15]William Baugh and Joe Stone, "Mobility and Wage Equilibrium in the Education Labor Market," Economics of Education Review 2 (Summer 1983): 253-74.

[16]Richard J. Murname, The Rhetoric and Reality of Merit Pay: Why Are They Different? (Palo Alto, Cal.: Institute for Research on Educational Finance and Governance, Stanford University, 1984), 10.

[17]Interview with Sally Haenelt, Committee Clerk, Senate Education Committee, Austin, Texas, February 13, 1985.

[18]Educational Research Service, Merit Pay Plans for Teachers, 17-20.

[19]Murname, Rhetoric and Reality of Merit Pay, 21-24.

[20]Interview with Dr. Thomas Murphy, Principal, Margo Elementary School, Weslaco ISD, Weslaco, Texas, January 10, 1985.

[21]Margaret Goertz, Ruth Ekstrom, and Richard Coley, The Impact of State Policy on Entrance into the Teaching Profession (Princeton: Division of Education Policy Research and Services, Educational Testing Service, October 1984).

[22]Governor Lamar Alexander, "Address to the Education Forum on Career Ladders," McGavock High School, Nashville, Tenn., July 27, 1984.

[23]Educational Research Service, Merit Pay Plans for Teachers, 62.

[24]Ibid., 61.

CHAPTER THREE
THE CONDUCT AND RESPONSIBILITIES OF STUDENTS

The recent criticisms of public education have almost universally cited declining test scores, diminishing proportions of school time spent in class, and increasing disciplinary problems as evidence of the need for immediate reform. As an example, A Nation at Risk cited a number of alarming statistics about student performance. Approximately 13 percent of all seventeen-year-olds in the United States are functionally illiterate. Among minority youth, the proportion may be as high as 40 percent. SAT scores from 1963 to 1980 reveal a virtually unbroken decline, although these scores have increased recently. Average verbal scores have decreased by over fifty points, and average math scores have decreased by nearly forty points over that seventeen-year period.[1] The average achievement of high school students on most standardized tests is now lower than it was twenty-eight years ago when Sputnik was launched and the last crisis in American education was declared. International comparisons of student achievement completed a decade ago indicate that, on nineteen academic tests, American students were never first or second and, in comparison with students from other industrialized nations, were ranked last on seven of the academic tests.

The National Commission on Excellence in Education and other critics have also decried the triviality of many secondary courses and charged that many students are substituting more "general" course offerings for the more challenging college preparatory and vocational education tracks. Students registering for general track courses increased from 12 percent in 1964 to 42 percent in 1978. Approximately 25 percent of the credits earned by high school students in a general track are in physical education, health, outside work experience, remedial English and math, and personal service and development courses.[2]

The authors of A Nation At Risk were also concerned that the educational system has lowered expectations of students. At the time the study was undertaken, no states required foreign language for graduation, thirty-five required only one year of math, and thirty-six required only one year of science; in thirteen states, 50 percent or more of the units required for graduation were electives.[3] Less homework, grade inflation, and more lenient college admission requirements serve as further examples of the lower standards.

Through House Bill 246, enacted in 1981 and analyzed in greater detail in chapter 9, the Texas state legislature addressed these and other concerns by increasing graduation requirements and incorporating the concept of mastery learning into the curricula. House Bill 72 continued the process of upgrading by including provisions governing student evaluation, promotion and retention, remediation, the place of cocurricular and extracurricular activities, and discipline. In contrast to the reforms examined in the previous chapter, which emphasize the requirements for teachers, these reforms delineate the responsibilities and requirements for students.

STUDENT EVALUATION AND TESTING

House Bill 72 requires that the Texas Education Agency adopt appropriate criterion-referenced tests to assess minimum competencies in reading, writing, and mathematics for all pupils at the first, third, fifth, seventh, and ninth grade levels; and in mathematics and English language arts for all pupils at the twelfth grade level. Beginning with the 1985-86 school year, Texas public schools will administer a battery of tests--the Texas Educational Assessment of Minimum Skills, or TEAMS--as well as a secondary level exit exam to see whether graduates are minimally competent.

The nationwide minimum competency testing (MCT) movement is an attempt to measure those basic skills needed for success as adults. If necessary, minimum competency tests are to be followed by remediation or by withholding of high school diplomas. Most of these tests are criterion-referenced, so that objectives are defined; students falling below some "acceptable" score are considered to have failed.[4] The MCT movement is really a revival of earlier practices. Through the early 1900s, promotion and graduation were determined by year-end examinations. By the late 1920s, however, the accumulation of a prescribed number of course credits in both major subjects and approved electives became an almost universal criterion for high school graduation in the United States.[5] The movement toward testing as the basis for awarding diplomas began in a few local systems in the 1960s; Oregon was the first state to adopt this policy in 1973.

Exit exams have been extensively challenged, especially on the ground that they discriminate against minority students who have themselves been discriminated against in schools. The most significant case pertaining to MCT involved a challenge to Florida's use of a functional literacy examination as a condition for receiving a high school diploma. In Debra P. v. Turlington, the plaintiffs asserted that their constitutional rights under the Fourteenth Amendment had been violated because of past discrimination, inadequate notice of a diploma sanction, and discrepancy between the test questions and actual classroom teaching. They also contended that remediation programs could lead to resegregation. The federal district court in Florida upheld the state's authority to establish academic requirements, including a test required for graduation. However, procedural issues, including Florida's implementation schedule, led the court to enjoin the state from withholding diplomas until all students tested had the benefit of a desegregated, twelve-year education, and all vestiges of intentional discrimination had been removed.[6]

The Fifth Circuit Court of Appeals upheld the suspension and introduced a new issue--content validity. The court ruled that students have a legitimate, state-created property right to education protected under the due process clause of the Fourteenth Amendment. Therefore, the right to a diploma had been abridged by inadequate notice of the test and inadequate time to prepare. In Anderson v. Banks, a Georgia federal district court decided in favor of a Georgia district that successfully established the validity of using the California Achievement Test results for awarding diplomas. But as in Debra P., the district could not immediately withhold diplomas because of procedural issues, and this case established a notification period of two years.[7] Thus, the courts have ruled that exit exams are constitutional if they meet the test of content validity, but that implementation must be postponed until all students have been taught in racially unified districts.

Practices in Other States

The results of minimum competency tests can be used for diagnostic and remedial purposes or for promotion and graduation. Approximately thirty-seven states have enacted legislation to require or permit competency testing for diagnosis, promotion, or graduation.[8] Currently, twenty states require passage of a MCT for high school graduation.[9] Several states permit some students (especially the handicapped) to earn diplomas by demonstrated proficiency on an alternative measure of basic skills.[10] Thirteen states require that districts offer remediation for students identified as deficient in basic skills. Only seven states have MCT programs which are developed, administered, and controlled by local districts.[11] The most popular model for MCT, therefore, is a single state-mandated set of competency testing procedures and standards. Almost all states that use MCT as a prerequisite for a diploma include reading, writing, and mathematics, and half the states focus solely on these subjects. Several states also test other "life skill" areas such as consumer knowledge and citizenship.[12]

Very few states have studied the outcomes of their MCT programs. The general pattern that emerged during the early period of testing (1975-79) was an initially high rate of failure followed by much lower rates of failure in subsequent testing.[13] The reasons for lower rates of failure from reexamination could include effective remediation and "teaching the test," as well as the fact that failure rates cannot account for those students who drop out or are ineligible for graduation due to other academic factors. States have been reluctant to report test performance for different groups of students. However, the evidence suggests higher failures among minorities. For instance, in North Carolina and California, diploma denials have been three to four times higher among black students than among white students.[14]

Testing in Texas

The TEAMS tests replace the Texas Assessment of Basic Skills (TABS), previously used to assess the progress of students. TEAMS tests first, seventh, eleventh, and twelfth graders in addition to the third, fifth, and ninth grade levels tested by TABS. The TEAMS test is more difficult than TABS, and the essential elements described in House Bill 246 will be more consciously incorporated in the test items.[15] The most important difference between TABS and TEAMS, however, is the requirement that students must pass the secondary level exit test in order to receive a high school diploma.

The Texas Education Agency, responsible for carrying out the entire assessment process, worked with Field Advisory Committees composed of Texas educators to refine essential objectives, measurement specifications, and questions to be included in the TEAMS tests. TEA contracted with a consulting firm, IOX Assessment Associates, to assist in the development of the TEAMS assessment instruments and has been further helped by the school districts and regional education service centers. Minority groups were apparently invited to monitor the test development process.[16] TEA conducted an instructional validity study during October 1984. Surveys were mailed to K-12 districts to obtain information on the appropriate level of an exit level exam, the extent to which instruction is being provided for designated skills, and any potential bias against minorities.

Based on the instructional validity study and the advice of educators, the State Board approved a list of objectives to be tested in math, reading, and writing. Test questions, written by IOX, were reviewed by TEA staff and Field Advisory Committees and then tested in a sample of school districts with approximately three thousand high school seniors. Based on analysis of these initial trials, staff from TEA and IOX developed four forms of the test, adopted by the State Board in June 1985.

Related provisions in House Bill 72 affecting TEAMS tests include exemptions, local options, comparison of results, and confidentiality. Students who have a physical or mental impairment or a learning disability that prevent them from mastering the basic skills assessed by TEAMS may be exempted. Local districts may elect to adopt and administer their own criterion or norm-referenced assessment instruments at any grade level, although these tests do not supersede the TEAMS tests. The bill requires TEA to analyze the results of locally adopted tests to compare the achievement of Texas students with students in other states. The SBOE and local districts must ensure the security of the instruments and tests in the preparation, administration, and grading. Meetings at which tests or test questions are discussed or adopted are closed to the public. The instruments, items, and tests are confidential, as are test scores for individual students.

Each school district must use the student performance data from basic skills and achievement tests to develop appropriate remedial instruction. This requirement ensures that the TEAMS tests are used to improve learning, rather than simply to classify students or to prevent incompetent students from graduating.

The cost of preparing, administering, and grading assessment instruments will be paid from state compensatory education funds. If a district does not receive compensatory aid, the commissioner of education will subtract the cost from the district's other foundation school fund allocations. This provision ensures that districts do not bypass administration of any tests required by House Bill 72.

Starting with the 1985-86 academic year, tenth graders will take the new exit level test. High school students will be given the opportunity to take the test twice in tenth grade and twice in eleventh grade. Seniors will have several opportunities to retake the test in their final year. Students who fail any portion of the test must retake it at each succeeding administration of the exit level test until they pass all sections.[17] Students at the first, third, fifth, seventh, and ninth grade levels will not be required to retake the respective TEAMS instrument or to perform satisfactorily to be promoted to the next grade level. Thus, satisfactory performance on a TEAMS test is a requirement for graduation, but not for promotion.

PROMOTION AND RETENTION

The issues of student evaluation and social promotion have generated some difficult questions about student achievement, the integrity and credibility of schools, teacher sovereignty, local control, and the effects of higher standards on minority groups and slow learners. House Bill 72 prohibits social promotion and declares that students may be promoted only on the basis of academic achievement. Students who have not maintained an average grade of 70 percent may not advance from one grade to the next, and students may not be given credit for a course in which they have a grade of under 70. Grades are reported for six-week intervals, and parents must sign student reports. The parents of students who fall below the 70 passing grade will receive a grade notice indicating that a parent/teacher conference is necessary.

Eventually, the State Board will require the mastery of essential elements--established in House Bill 246, analyzed in chapter 9--to determine academic achievement. In the 1984-85 school year, course credit and grade level advancement were based on numerical scores. Beginning with the 1985-86 school year, however, mastery of the essential elements for each subject or course will be a prerequisite for course credit and advancement.[18]

SBOE does make an exception to the prohibition of social promotion. In grades one through eight, districts may promote students with averages below 70 if the district has determined that a student is achieving at his or her maximum ability and if the student has participated in tutorials with no apparent benefit. Furthermore, the student placed at the next grade cannot be achieving at a level that is significantly lower than other students at that grade level, and placement cannot disrupt or overly complicate instruction for other students or the teacher. The district must also fully inform the parent or guardian that the student was not promoted but placed at the next grade level.[19] Exceptions to social promotion are not made for high school (ninth through twelfth grades). Clearly, this exception should be relatively difficult to apply, and thus confirms the opposition of the Texas legislature to social promotion.

In practice, actual retention will probably be limited. SBOE has ruled that no students shall be required to repeat any grade level more than one time. Also, no student shall be required to repeat any grade level if that student has repeated two different grade levels previously.[20] Because retention applies to grade levels and not individual courses, this option is not applicable to high school students.

Although local district policies vary, the general pattern is that districts engage in social promotion at the elementary grade levels and somewhat less often at the junior high level. Usually, however, the practice of social promotion ends with high school. Districts rarely allow retention in any grade for more than one consecutive year. The prevalent notion among the districts we interviewed is that holding back a student for more than one year is detrimental to all concerned, and many districts place a cap on the number of times a student may be retained in his or her career.

Districts agree that teachers can control grades by setting the content of tests at any level of difficulty they wish: tests and quizzes can be as difficult or simple as teachers want. To a large extent, therefore, teachers will determine the effectiveness of the state's new restrictions on social promotion and course credit by the extent to which they exercise their power to set grades. The teachers and administrators we interviewed agreed that it would be impossible to eliminate all social promotion through legislation because of the power of teachers. However, they all agreed that the prohibition will have some effect on social promotion, since it establishes an important norm. House Bill 72 also makes teachers more accountable to the district, state, and public through the assignment of numerical grades and enables principals to see whether teachers are consistently inflating or deflating grades.

Teachers and administrators also agree that some social promotion is necessary. For example, when intermediate schools promote sixteen-year-olds to high school who have never passed the eighth grade, problems arise and the students usually drop out. An emphasis on maintaining high standards for promotion may undermine the efforts to encourage marginal students to remain in school. In addition, overage students can create serious discipline problems and distract other students, particularly in lower grade levels. These practical considerations, as well as the stigma associated with retention, must be balanced against the integrity and credibility of the public school system.

House Bill 72 requires the State Board of Education to establish alternatives to social promotion for students who are consistently unable to be promoted because of poor academic achievement. This area has caused a great deal of confusion and anxiety for districts. The alternatives include special remedial support, including tutorials, summer school, specialized teaching, and instruction by experts outside the school; an ungraded, continuous progress class where students are grouped by ability in a classroom which provides the essential elements for all subjects; and a nongraded continuous progress class for those basic subjects where students do not meet standards.

The summer school option allows a final grade to be postponed until the requirements of the course are completed, during a summer school program. At the option of the local districts, summer school programs may be offered for any subject or course, at any grade level, for whatever length of time is necessary for students to satisfy course requirements.[21]

The continuous progress class is an ungraded program in which instruction is based on progress through the sequence of essential elements, concentrating on English language arts and mathematics.[22] These classes emphasize progress rather than mastery of essential elements. This kind of instructional arrangement applies to students in grades one through eight, and parents must be consulted before students may participate.

At the ninth through twelfth grade levels, social promotion does not really apply, because students must register and receive credit for individual courses and because many are past the age of compulsory attendance. The summer school option, however, is available for those high school students who are failing a course. In addition, a pass/fail option, while not a true alternative to social promotion, is designed to encourage students to take more than the twenty-one units required for graduation. At the student's option, letter or numerical grades will not appear on his or her transcript or be calculated in the cumulative average.[23]

So far, the criteria for defining alternatives to social promotion are fairly stringent, and local districts may need more options and flexibility in handling individual cases. The costs of establishing these different alternative programs are at least partially paid through state compensatory education funding. However, some alternatives to social promotion are impractical for districts below a certain size, and tutorials may be the only feasible alternative for small districts. The demand for summer school programs may be too low to justify their operation. Similarly, creating continuous progress classes for different grade levels and subject areas may be too costly and logistically complicated for the districts. While districts have established tutorials (as described below), they have so far done little to establish continuous progress classes or summer school programs, and they have been given little guidance from the state level in this unfamiliar area.

STUDENT REMEDIATION: TUTORIALS

House Bill 72 and Chapter 75 (analyzed in chapter 9) complement one another in the area of tutorials, as House Bill 72 requires tutorials to complement the House Bill 246 curriculum requirements. In addition, tutorials are necessary to ease the transition for students to the more stringent promotion and graduation requirements in House Bill 72.

House Bill 72 requires that each district provide tutorials. Although tutorials may be voluntary, a student whose grade in a subject is lower than 70 attends tutorials during the following reporting period twice a week or more, as determined by the district. A district is not required to provide transportation to students who attend tutorials.

The State Board has set a number of standards for tutorial programs. Districts must offer tutorials at least two days per week for a cumulative total of ninety minutes. Tutorials can be scheduled before, during, or after school, in the evening, and on weekends; and districts may offer shorter sessions (less than forty-five minutes) during more days of the week. Students must not be assigned to tutorials which cause them to miss classroom instruction.   Districts must offer tutorials in English language arts, math, science, and social studies and may elect to provide sessions in other subject.   Grade reports notify parents whether a student is recommended or required to attend tutorials during the next six-week grading period.   The forty-five-minute planning and preparation period required for each teacher during the school day cannot be used for tutorial purposes, and districts may require a minimum amount of tutorial participation as part of the regular contractual duties of all teachers.[24]

Practices and Experiences of Districts

Although teachers and administrators endorse the concept of remediation in principle, the general consensus of the districts interviewed is that tutorials have not been very effective, and attendance has been disappointingly low.   The reasons include some inherent problems with the tutorial concept, the "noncommittal" nature of the bill's language, and implementation problems at the district level. The lack of parental support and the lack of funding for transportation, different kinds of instructional materials designed for remediation, personnel, and space have discouraged many districts from requiring mandatory attendance for eligible students.   Most districts send notes to parents informing them of their child's eligibility and require a signed release form from parents before allowing student participation.   Students who are not failing but elect to attend the tutorial sessions are allowed to do so in most districts, because attendance levels are so low among failing students. Most districts report a better response among elementary students than among secondary students, presumably because parents are more attentive to their childrens' performance at the grade level, and elementary students are failing grade levels, not individual courses.

Administrators report that attendance in tutorials was low in 1984-85. Under these conditions, the effectiveness of tutorial programs is doubtful. Tutoring can help some students, but for others there is an inherent flaw: students who perform poorly because they dislike school or are unmotivated are unlikely to learn simply by having more of the same kind of education.   Where tutorials are required, students may view them as punishment rather than opportunities to learn. In still other cases, teachers report the students fail because of a lack of basic skills such as reading, yet tutorials generally do not emphasize study skills or reading. (For students who lack basic skills, an alternative to the existing tutorials is to require that failing students attend classes in basic reading, math, and study skills.)

One principal expressed the fear that, with tutorials now required, teachers will no longer tutor their own students as they have in the past. Some districts are attempting to develop a tutorial program that keeps teachers with their original students.   This type of arrangement is particularly important at the lower grades, where younger students and their teachers develop special relationships.

Some districts require attendance unless the parents sign a form to the effect that they do not wish their child to participate--and many do not. However, most districts have made tutorials optional, and participation has been relatively low. Parents and students may not take tutorials seriously in districts that do not require them. There are often more tangible barriers as well. One is the lack of transportation. Another is that the pupil/teacher ratios are too high due to a shortage of teachers, partly because many teachers are not anxious to continue teaching after school.

In most districts teacher participation is voluntary and response has been low. Tutorial programs have posed a hardship for teachers in districts which require teacher participation or provide no compensation. Although the vast majority of the districts interviewed are paying their teachers overtime at an hourly rate (usually $10), those districts that are not compensating teachers for tutorials have experienced some problems with teacher morale.

The interviews revealed a number of other issues related to tutorials. In those districts where students are ability-grouped beginning in the lower grades, teachers of low-ability classes are especially burdened by tutorials. Science, math, reading, and language arts teachers have been disproportionately affected by the tutorial provisions of House Bill 72, since these are areas with required sessions and high failure rates. One unclear aspect of the bill, and an area in which SBOE has not issued any specific interpretations, is whether a certified teacher participating in the tutorial program may only tutor in the field in which he or she is certified.

In districts where tutorial teaching is voluntary and few regular teachers participate, some districts have resorted to hiring substitute teachers, retired teachers, and student tutors. These tutors' salaries are lower than the hourly rate for regular teachers. Another advantage is that "outsiders" often have more energy and fresh approaches. In several districts, high school students (such as National Honor Society members) are paid minimum wage to co-tutor in a structured tutorial program at all grade levels.

The State Board has passed a ruling that districts may conduct tutorials during the school day to avoid the problems of teacher participation, student attendance, lack of transportation, and compensation. However, this arrangement has cut into valuable teacher preparation time in some districts, even though SBOE has ruled that this should not be allowed to occur.

In summary, the tutorial program now suffers from a variety of logistical and financial problems, as well as from some flaws in the basic conception of more school for students who have not done well. The logistics of implementing a tutorial program are especially complicated in small districts with limited staff resources. Additional experimentation with remedial programs may be necessary in order to develop the most effective approaches.

STUDENT TIME

House Bill 72 contains several provisions to make sure that students spend time on schoolwork, rather than on activities unrelated to education. A new absence rule requires that a student cannot be given credit for a class if he or she has more than five days of unexcused absence during a semester. Excused absences include student sickness, medical and dental appointments, sickness or death in the family, quarantine, observation of holy days, weather or road conditions making travel dangerous, or any other usual causes acceptable to teachers, principals, or superintendents. The reason for a student absence must be stated in writing and signed by the parent or guardian.[25]

The State Board has tentatively ruled that a student can compensate for absences in order to receive course credit. If a student attends class outside the regular school day for at least 150 percent of the time that he or she was absent and prepares written material demonstrating mastery of the material presented during the absence, the unexcused absence will be changed to "present" for purposes of course credit. Upon reduction of the number of unexcused absences to three or less, the student may receive course credit.[26]

The main issues revolving around the new absence restrictions concern local district control. Some districts have expressed the conviction that the district should determine whether an absence is excused. For example, in Roosevelt ISD, a committee of teachers and administrators has decided whether excess absences were permissible or not.[27] The latest ruling by SBOE is that a student must be truant for an absence to be unexcused;[28] therefore, parents may remove their children from class for any reason.

Another effort in House Bill 72 to focus school activities on instructional time is a new restriction on extracurricular and cocurricular activities. These provisions are the most controversial of student-related issues and will require the greatest monitoring.

The State Board defines cocurricular activities as extensions of classroom instruction in which an entire class (or a significant portion) participates. Cocurricular activities occur during the regular school day and should enhance student learning of essential elements through participation, demonstration, illustration, and observation. Cocurricular activities are included in the teacher's instructional plan and are supervised by a teacher or other educational professional such as a librarian, school nurse, counselor, or administrator.[29] Examples of cocurricular activities include field trips to museums, planetariums, and performing arts exhibits. Extracurricular activities generally occur outside the regular school day and are only indirectly related to the curriculum. Examples of extracurricular activities include band, sports, and student organizations.

To limit interruptions of the school day and participation in extracurricular activities, SBOE has handed down ten-day and eight-hour rules.

The ten-day rule limits interruptions during the school day for extracurricular and cocurricular activities to ten per year for any student. TEA will grant up to a five-day extension for those students who qualify for a higher level of competition. The eight-hour rule limits practice, performance, and travel time outside the regular school day during the regular school week (excluding weekends) to eight hours a week for each activity. TEA will grant exemptions from this rule for a limited number of circumstances.[30]

A relatively recent SBOE ruling stipulates the number of hours that must be earned by seventh through twelfth graders in order to participate in extracurricular activities. In the seventh through ninth grades, students must have regularly passed the preceding grade level or have received credit for all but one course required in the previous grade. Students in the tenth through twelfth grades must have earned at least four, nine, and fifteen credits, respectively, toward graduation.

The best-known and most controversial SBOE ruling is the six week rule, also known as the "no-pass no-play" rule. This excludes those students who earn below a 70 in any course from participating in extracurricular activities during the following grading period. Students remain eligible for practice during the probationary six weeks, although participation is prohibited. A principal may waive a suspension if the class is an honors or advanced class.

In the spring of 1985, many students affected by the "no-pass no-play" rule challenged its constitutionality in state court; about 35 lawsuits were filed. In the Houston area, a state district judge issued a temporary injunction blocking several school districts from enforcing the rule. However, in July 1985 the State Supreme Court upheld the rule, stating that "a student's right to participate in extracurricular activities does not rise to the same level as the right to free speech or free exercise of religion."[31] While this outcome is unlikely to be overturned, the amount of litigation is indicative of how controversial the "no-pass no-play" rule has been.

District Practices and Community Reactions

The suspicion that time in extracurricular activities was overwhelming academic work--the "tail wagging the dawg"--motivated the legislation about student time. The Texas legislature felt that relatively drastic action was necessary to get the attention of school districts. However, the restrictions on extracurricular activities have become emotionally charged political issues at the community level. During the winter and spring of 1985, as the effects of the "no-pass no-play" rule first appeared, Texas newspapers were filled with stories of students unable to show their prize heifers, of bands and basketball teams decimated, of debate teams unable to travel to competitions because of the "no-pass no-play" rule and restrictions on absences. Criticism from parents and students involved in agricultural activities has been particularly vehement, because they can no longer leave school to enter their livestock in county fairs and other shows.

Although the legislation and rulings have imposed consistency on the districts, many districts have been uncertain how to implement the requirement, to distinguish cocurricular from extracurricular activities, or to determine student eligibility. Moreover, local administrators have had to justify to their local communities the actions of the legislature and the State Board. Because House Bill 72 did not specify how cocurricular and extracurricular activities should be limited, the burden of scheduling and record keeping has fallen on districts. (Although SBOE did not require standard recordkeeping in 1984-85, it will review the experiences of districts to gather ideas for more specific guidelines.)[32]

Many administrators and teachers feel that the "no-pass no-play" rule may be too rigid for good students who fail only one course. Many districts agree that the State Board should revise this provision to require an average grade of 70 for the entire year or a certain percentage of the courses passed with a 70. Districts also assert that the period of exclusion from extracurricular activities should be limited to one week rather than the entire six-week grading period; excluding an athlete from competition for six weeks, for example, effectively ends his or her ability to play for an entire season.

In order to comply with the ten-day rule, which covers cocurricular as well as extracurricular activities, districts have had to reduce assemblies of students during the school day. (Chapter 75, examined in chapter 9, has also cut into cocurricular activities.) Despite complaints about the stringency of the rulings concerning student time, most administrators and teachers welcome the new requirements as ways of getting students back in classrooms. Sometimes, they view the requirements of House Bill 72 as ways of reducing pressures from their communities to dilute the curriculum: they can blame the legislature for the new ruling and therefore deflect hostility about extracurricular activities toward Austin. The provisions about extracurricular issues may need to be adjusted, as experiences accumulate in the next year or two, but most educators still feel it has been a step in the direction of restoring education to the schools.

STUDENT DISCIPLINE

One of the issues that has emerged in the recent examinations of American education is student discipline. The opinion has become more common that schools--especially high schools--have become unruly and sometimes lawless places, and tales of violence and drug dealing are often told. The Select Committee on Public Education heard testimony about discipline in the schools and recommended a discipline management program.

In House Bill 72 the state legislature promulgated an extremely comprehensive, detailed, and stringent set of provisions regarding the role of local districts in discipline management. The bill requires each district to develop a a discipline management program based on draft rules and a suggested format provided by TEA.[33]

House Bill 72 and SBOE rules outline four issues which must be addressed in a discipline management plan: student conduct, the responsibilities of parents, due process procedures, and the duties of campus discipline officials. At a minimum, the student code of conduct must include rules, regulations, and expectations related to conduct; the consequences of violating the code and the conditions for which discipline, removal to an alternative educational setting, or expulsion may be imposed; definitions of serious and persistent misbehavior and incorrigible conduct; an outline of the district's alternative educational program; and procedures for communicating and distributing the code to students, parents, and teachers.[34] The legislature and State Board emphasize the importance of parents in the school's disciplinary process. At least two parent/teacher conferences must be held during the school year for the parents of students who have committed one or more disciplinary infractions or who have been removed to an alternative educational program at least once during the previous or current semester. Districts must also provide parent training workshops for home reinforcement of study skills and specific curriculum objectives. Finally, districts must provide annually for signed statements by each student's parent that the parent understands and consents to the responsibilities outlined in the district's Student Code of Conduct.[35]

Teacher Training Programs in Discipline Management

Each district must provide training for its administrators, counselors, campus discipline personnel, and professional and support staff of alternative education programs in the discipline management plan of the district.[36] Districts must use in-service workshops for reinforcing teacher training in discipline management and must verify to TEA that each teacher in the district has received training in the district's discipline management plan by December 31, 1986.

Alternative Education Program

House Bill 72 provides for removing students from the classroom in order to maintain effective discipline. It allows short-term suspensions (one to three days) without declaring the student incorrigible and removal of an incorrigible pupil to an alternative education program.[37] To declare a pupil guilty of incorrigible conduct, a hearing that provides procedural due process must find either that the pupil's continued presence in school presents a clear, present, and continuing danger of physical harm to him or her or to other individuals or that the pupil has engaged in serious or persistent misbehavior which violates specific published standards of student conduct for the school district and that all reasonable alternatives (including a variety of discipline management techniques) have been exhausted.

Alternative education programs fall into two categories: supervised and unsupervised educational settings. Supervised educational settings include in-school suspension, reassignment of classes, transfer to a different campus, transfer to a school-community guidance center, and assignment to a community-based alternative school. Unsupervised educational settings usually involve home-based instruction, but students removed for truancy and tardiness cannot be placed in an unsupervised educational setting. The length of removal to an alternative educational setting is limited. Local school boards can also recommend disciplinary action for pupils who accrue more than five days of unexcused absences during a semester or ten during a school year. A pupil's parent or a representative is entitled to participate in a disciplinary proceeding. SBOE rules provide a great deal of detail about the procedures before, during, and after a hearing.

Expulsions

House Bill 72 stated that no student shall be expelled from school unless he or she has assaulted a teacher or other individual on school property and, in the opinion of the local school board, the student's continued presence presents a clear and continuing danger of physical harm to the student or to other individuals on school property. Alternatively, a student may be expelled if he or she has been moved to an alternative education program; has continued to be guilty of incorrigible conduct to the extent that keeping the student in the program or the schools would seriously impair the ability to provide for other students; and no further reasonable efforts to provide for the continuing education of the student can be made.

The criteria in House Bill 72 for finding a pupil incorrigible, removing a student to an alternative education program, and expelling a student are extremely stringent and complicated. The new suspension rules affect mainly secondary schools, because districts report that elementary level students are rarely suspended. The positive effects of the discipline management program are greater consistency within and among districts and a greater awareness among teachers and students of district expectations. Parents have been more fully integrated into the discipline process through the specification of parental duties and responsibilities. Teachers, administrators, and other school personnel are receiving formal training in discipline management techniques and the plans of their district. Procedures of due process have been standardized, and much of the previous arbitrariness in suspension and expulsion has been eliminated. Most importantly, however, students in trouble are kept in supervised educational settings, interruption of instructional time is minimized, and students sustain no academic penalty for disciplinary infractions. The new requirements have also forced teachers to put their rules and regulations into writing and communicate them to students and parents. Principals review these classroom rules and can therefore change any practices inconsistent with the district's adopted program.

However, most districts agree that House Bill 72 and the SBOE rules have taken the power away from the local school boards to suspend and to expel problem students. Many administrators feel that the conditions for suspension and expulsion in House Bill 72 are too narrow, and districts resent having to declare students incorrigible to suspend them, because some individual actions by students who are not incorrigible--drug and weapons violations, for example--may warrant suspension or expulsion. Most district administrators feel that decisions on discipline management should be made at the local level. Because of the volume of criticism of the discipline management sections in House Bill 72, House Bill 408, sponsored by Representative Bill

Haley, was introduced during the 1985 legislative session, superseding the discipline management programs in House Bill 72. The bill liberalized certain aspects of House Bill 72, such as what teachers can do in the classroom and short-term suspensions, provided more detailed definitions of incorrigibility, and also addressed the handling of such serious infractions as possession of drugs, alcohol, and weapons. Despite widespread support from administrators and teachers and passage in the House, the bill did not pass the Senate because of procedural differences; therefore, no changes in the discipline management programs were enacted.

Funding

Discipline management involves more time, more people, and more paperwork than past discipline practices. Many districts have had to hire additional personnel to supervise students referred to alternative education programs. Space may prove to be a problem for some districts. Although the costs of establishing alternative programs are high, House Bill 72 makes no provision for funding such programs. One district we interviewed received a grant from the Criminal Justice Department to set up an alternative school,[38] but otherwise districts must fund such programs from local revenues.

CONCLUSIONS

In House Bill 72, the state established a set of minimum standards related to promotion, graduation, remediation, eligibility for extracurricular activities, and discipline. In particular, the legislature and SBOE have adopted a new graduation policy requiring passage of a minimum competency exam, as well as increased academic requirements and grading standards. The aim of these reforms is to motivate students, ensure a minimum level of competency, and identify students in need of remediation.

The general consensus of educators is that the provisions in House Bill 72 cannot completely eliminate social promotion in Texas schools. But some promotion will be eliminated, and as a result many administrators feel that dropout rates may double or even triple; those students who anticipate failure on the exit level test may drop out as well. Some educators claim that the new passing grade has already increased the dropout rate, especially among minorities.[39] This result would be unfortunate, because the intent of House Bill 72 is to prevent students from graduating without basic skills and to provide remedial instruction, not to push students out of school. Yet, ironically, as public expectations about student performance rise, dropout rates may increase.

Many educators fear that minority students will be disproportionately affected by the provisions of House Bill 72. Because of experiences in other states, some fear that minority students will be more likely to fail the exit exam. In fact, some experiences in Texas districts have already confirmed this danger. For example, Austin ISD reported higher failure rates for black and Hispanic students on the TEAMS tests given to juniors and seniors in spring 1985.[40]   In addition, many minority students may be eliminated from extracurricular activities due to the new passing grade, which might contribute to more attrition and discipline problems. Thus, the overall effect of these reforms could be discriminatory, even if the intent is not.

Furthermore, stricter grading standards could cause additional problems for slow learners.   Some students may not be capable of passing through the system with a 70, even with remediation, yet there must be a way to pass those who are not eligible for special education. This is especially a concern at the elementary level, because some administrators feel that primary schools may lose their capacity to adjust teaching content and practice to slower students.

Another problem that has been realized by some administrators is that the more serious, college-bound students have been taking easier courses because of the minimum passing grade and are sometimes reluctant to register for advanced or honors courses. The dilemma is that measures designed to motivate better performance may instead have the opposite effect.

There are, then, several ironies in the provisions of House Bill 72 related to student conduct.   Measures designed to improve education may instead dilute it or push marginal students out of school. To prevent these unintended results, it will be necessary to monitor the effects of House Bill 72 on student performance, to devise effective strategies for remediation, and to ensure that the potentially punitive aspects are softened by its supportive intentions.

Notes

[1]National Commission on Excellence in Education, A Nation At Risk: The Imperative for Educational Reform (Washington, D.C.: U.S. Government Printing Office, April 1983), 5.

[2]Ibid., 19.

[3]Ibid., 20.

[4]Jeri J. Goldman, "Political and Legal Issues in Minimum Competency Testing," Educational Forum 48, no. 2 (Winter 1984): 207.

[5]Robert C. Serow, "Current Trends in States' Graduation Policies," Integrated Education 21 (January-December 1983): 93.

[6]Martha M. McCarthy, "Minimum Competency Testing for Students: Educational and Legal Issues," Educational Horizons 61, no. 3 (Spring 1983): 105-6.

[7]Ibid.

[8]Antonette Logar, "Minimum Competency Testing in Schools: Legislative Action and Judicial Review," Journal of Law and Education 13, no. 1 (January 1984): 38.

[9]Serow, "Current Trends," 93.

[10]Robert C. Serow, "Effects of Minimum Competency Testing for Minority Students: A Review of Expectations and Outcomes," Urban Review 16, no. 2 (1984): 68.

[11]Goldman, "Political and Legal Issues," 209.

[12]McCarthy, "Minimum Competency Testing," 104.

[13]Serow, "Current Trends," 94.

[14]Ibid.

[15]Interview with Gayle Micholson, Educational Program Director, Texas Education Agency, Austin, Texas, March 20, 1985.

[16]Texas Education Agency, "Executive Summary of the Texas Assessment of Basic Skills, Report of the 1984 Assessment," undated. Although this document claims that minority groups, including the Mexican American Legal Defense and Education Fund (MALDEF), were invited to comment, in fact MALDEF was never contacted; oral communication, Pat Longoria, MALDEF, July 18, 1985.

[17]Interview with Gayle Micholson, March 20, 1985.

[18]19 Texas Administrative Code, Sec. 75.193.

[19]Texas Education Agency, "Promotion and Alternatives to Social Promotion" (presented to the State Board of Education, Austin, Texas, October 19, 1984), 4.

[20]Ibid.

[21]19 Texas Administrative Code, Sec. 75.192.

[22]Texas Education Agency, "Promotion and Alternatives," 3.

[23]19 Texas Administrative Code, Sec. 75.194.

[24]19 Texas Administrative Code, Sec. 75.173.

[25]Texas Education Code, Sec. 21.035. Religious observation (including travel time) is counted as attendance for school funding purposes. Likewise, students who are absent during the official roll call due to participation in cocurricular and/or extracurricular activities are counted present for funding purposes. Medical and dental appointments do not qualify, however.

[26]Proposed State Board of Education Ruling on Texas Education Code, Sec. 21.041.

[27]Interview with Mike Moehler, Elementary School Principal, Alvarado ISD, Alvarado, Texas, November 29, 1984.

[28]Interview with Ted Ewing, Elementary School Principal, Roosevelt ISD, Roosevelt, Texas, January 25, 1985.

[29]Proposed amendment to 19 Texas Administrative Code, Sec. 97.113.

[30]Texas Education Code Sec. 21.920.

[31]Mike Hailey, "High Court Upholds Rule on 'No Play'," Austin American-Statesman, July 11, 1985.

[32]Interview with Jim Clark, Director of School Liaison, Texas Education Agency, Austin, Texas, March 20, 1985.

[33]Interview with Tommy Harns, Education Program Director, Department of Planning and Research, Texas Education Agency, Austin, Texas, March 20, 1985.

[34]Proposed amendment to 19 Texas Administrative Code, Chapter 133, Subchapter B.

[35]Texas Education Code, Sec. 21.702.

[36]Proposed amendment to 19 Texas Administrative Code Chapter 133, Subchapter B.

[37]Ibid.

[38]Interview with Dr. Arnold D. Oates, Jr., Superintendent, Brazosport ISD, Brazosport, Texas, January 25, 1985.

[39]Interview by Peter McCanna and John Zapata with Dr. Forrest E. Watson, Superintendent, Hurst-Euless-Bedford ISD, Bedford, Texas, January 25, 1985.

[40]"Minimum Competency for Graduation," 1984-85 Final Report, Office of Research and Evaluation, Publication 84.59, Austin ISD, July 15, 1985.

CHAPTER FOUR
STATE-FUNDED COMPENSATORY EDUCATION

The concept of "compensatory education" arose in the early 1960s as part of the movement to eliminate poverty. The architects of the War on Poverty viewed education as critical to breaking the "cycle of poverty." They believed the failure of poor children to do as well in school as their middle-class peers was an important factor perpetuating that cycle.

In this view, the children of the poor are no less intelligent than the children of the middle class; therefore, differences in their achievement in school must be due to adverse environmental factors. Advocates of compensatory education do not always agree on the precise nature of these environmental factors but tend to lump them together under the general label "educational deprivation." The phrase "compensatory education" comes from the need to "compensate" for the low-income child's environmental disadvantages by offering more intensive instruction.

The two major federal compensatory education programs established in the mid-1960s, Head Start and Title I of the Elementary and Secondary Education Act, sought to provide additional educational services to the children of the poor. Head Start offered preschool programs, while Title I funded programs of intensive help for low-achieving students in schools with above-average concentrations of low-income children. School districts in Texas received approximately $200 million a year from the federal government to operate programs under the successor to Title I, Chapter 1 of the Education Consolidation and Improvement Act of 1981. In practice, federal compensatory education money serves students who are falling behind in basic skills such as reading or mathematics and whose learning deficit is not due to any identifiable physical or mental handicap or to inability to speak English. These funds are allocated to districts based on the number of low-income students in the district, measured by a count of students eligible for free or reduced-price school lunches.

There has been considerable debate about the effectiveness of compensatory programs. In the early years of Title I, funds were often used for purposes unrelated to compensatory learning, and educators were unsure what compensatory programs should be; under these conditions it is not surprising that evaluations of Title I programs found few positive effects. In the past decade, as abuses have diminished and methods have improved, the evaluations have shown more systematic positive effects;[1] in particular, the most sophisticated analysis--the Sustaining Effects Study, designed to see whether compensatory programs have lasting rather than temporary gains--has confirmed improvements in math for all elementary grades and in reading for grades one to three.[2] As in so many other areas of education, then, well-designed compensatory programs can provide real benefits to disadvantaged children, although many ineffective programs persist as well.

Before House Bill 72, the amount of funding for state compensatory education (SCE) was much smaller than that for the federal program. Texas districts received an allocation of $44 per low-income child, or a total of approximately $51.6 million in state compensatory funding in the 1983-84 school year, about one-quarter of the federal funds. Low-income children in SCE were, and still are, counted by the same method used for the federal program. The legislature made a separate appropriation for SCE every biennium; the law provided that, if appropriations were insufficient to provide $44 per child, this allotment was to be reduced by the percentage of the shortfall.

House Bill 72 changed this funding mechanism by making state compensatory education part of a district's total foundation allotment, supplying 1.2 times the normal adjusted basic allotment for each low-income child. The extra 20 percent was counted as the district's compensatory education allotment. For large districts, this extra 20 percent amounted to 20 percent of $1,290 or $258 in 1984-85, considerably higher than the prior allocation of $44 per child; for high-cost districts, the amount of SCE funds was higher still.[3] This change in formula resulted in more than a sixfold increase in the state compensatory education funding for Texas school districts, to approximately $320 million for the 1984-85 school year.

DIFFERENCES BETWEEN FEDERAL AND STATE COMPENSATORY EDUCATION

Districts face much less formal restriction on how they can spend their SCE funds than they do for money received under Chapter 1. Unlike federal funds, the money can be used to offer services to the general student population, to provide English as a Second Language and bilingual services, and to pay for services to some students that the district provides to other students with noncompensatory education funds. The differences between state and federal compensatory funding include the following:

- School Selection: A district is allowed to spend state compensatory education money in any school. Chapter 1 money can only be spent in "eligible" schools, which means, with certain exceptions specifically provided for in the law, schools with a higher-than-district-average number or percentage of low-income students.

- Student Selection: The federal program requires districts to use a formal and systematic process for identifying which students are to receive services, and districts can not offer Chapter 1 services to any student who had not been identified by this process. In addition, the district is required to serve the children identified as being in greatest need of Chapter 1 services before serving anyone else. By contrast, a district can offer SCE-funded services to its entire student body or to any student that someone in the district decides is in need of remediation. This gives districts great flexibility to use state compensatory education money for almost any remediation-related purpose and makes SCE a logical funding source for tutorials or other remedial programs serving a rapidly changing group of students. On the other hand, this flexibility may have led to districts' spreading the money too thinly to offer students the intensity of services they need.

- Grade Levels Served: Approximately 80 percent of Chapter 1 dollars in Texas are spent on children in the preschool and elementary grades, in the belief that remediation is most effective when begun early. By contrast, SCE funds seem to be divided more evenly between the elementary and secondary levels. The increased number of classes required for high school graduation and Chapter 75's restrictions on pulling students out of regular classes are likely to reinforce the tendency to concentrate Chapter 1 money in the elementary grades. In contrast, the state high school graduation requirement that students pass the Texas Educational Assessment of Minimum Skills test may have led to an increased expenditure of SCE funds in secondary grades to help students who failed the test.

- Accountability: Chapter 1 requires districts to offer programs "of sufficient size, scope, and quality to give reasonable promise of substantial progress toward meeting the special educational needs of the children being served"; to evaluate their programs by methods including "objective measurements of educational achievement in basic skills"; and to use the results of the evaluation to make necessary improvements in the program.[4] This evaluation requirement has generated an immense volume of literature attempting to document the effectiveness of different approaches to compensatory education. In contrast, districts receiving state compensatory education money are not required to demonstrate the effectiveness of their programs.

Before receiving Chapter 1 funds, a district is required to describe to the state what it plans to do with the money, in an application that is usually twenty or thirty pages long. Districts receive SCE funds automatically if they qualify for state aid and fill in a one-page form at the end of the year on how they spent the money. Federal compensatory education programs are monitored more systematically by the state than are state compensatory education programs. The Texas Education Agency employed twenty-three full-time individuals specifically for on-site monitoring of Chapter 1 programs.[5] State compensatory education programs are not monitored and are not examined systematically in TEA's accreditation audits.[6]

- Administrative Costs: Up to 35 percent of state compensatory education money can be spent on administrative costs directly or indirectly related to the district's remedial program. Since this concept of indirect administrative costs is interpreted rather loosely, in practice any district that wants to spend the full 35 percent on administrative costs can do so. Chapter 1 is much stricter about which administrative costs are allowed to be allocated to the program, in order to prevent districts from using federal funds to cover ordinary administrative costs. The state allows districts an indirect cost rate based on the proportion of the district's overall budget spent on administration, usually around 3 to 5 percent.

- Chapter 1's Supplement-Not-Supplant Requirement: Districts are permitted to use Chapter 1 money only as a supplement, to provide more intensive educational services to Chapter 1 children than other children receive. Districts are not allowed to use Chapter 1 compensatory funds to pay for services that they provided to other students out of noncompensatory education funds or that are mandated by state law. In the language of the statute, to do so would constitute "supplanting," or using Chapter 1 money to replace state or local spending that occurs anyway. State compensatory education has no supplement-not-supplant requirement, so state compensatory funds can be used to replace local spending on remedial programs and to pay for a broad range of services that the district would provide with local funds if the state money were absent.

- Parent Involvement: Federal law requires that Chapter 1 programs be "designed and implemented in consultation with parents and teachers" and that school districts "convene annually a public meeting, to which all parents of eligible students shall be invited, to explain to parents the programs and activities provided with funds made available under this chapter."[7] Although this requirement is a weakening of the federal parent involvement requirement from the days of Title I, it is still strong by comparison with state compensatory education, which contains no parent involvement requirement whatsoever.

In general, the restrictiveness of the federal money encourages districts to pinpoint those students in greatest need of remediation, to provide those students with educational services that are significantly more intensive than those provided to the general student population, and to keep track of whether the remedial program is actually working. In addition, the supplement-not-supplant requirement makes the federal dollars more likely to increase the level of spending. On the other hand, restrictiveness may in some instances lead to rigidity and to districts' preferring old program designs because they are known to be legal and secure from audit exceptions, not because they consider them to be the most effective. The flexibility of state compensatory education may encourage districts to use the money to try out new programs that they would not have attempted in the presence of complex legal requirements.

CHANGES IN STATE COMPENSATORY EDUCATION UNDER HOUSE BILL 72

House Bill 72 made several changes in the requirements for how districts spend their state compensatory education money and report those expenditures to the state. Prior to House Bill 72, the law required districts to administer a state-adopted criterion-referenced test to third, fifth, and ninth grade students, in addition to any students in the tenth through twelfth grades who had failed to pass the ninth grade test. Each district was required to use the results of the state test "to design and implement appropriate compensatory instructional services for students" and to "submit an annual report to the commissioner of education which describes how state compensatory funds received pursuant to this section have been used to provide for those services."[8] House Bill 72 added two new subsections requiring remediation for any student who failed part or all of the high school exit exam or whose TEAMS score was "below a standard established by the State Board of Education."

In practice, this report was a one-page form which provided very little information on how the district had actually used the money, depending on how the district filled out the report. There were no additional requirements about what "appropriate" compensatory services might have consisted of, such as the "size, scope, and quality" requirements in the federal Chapter 1 program.

Moreover, there was no direct monitoring by the state of how districts spent their state compensatory education allotment. The logical agency to monitor districts' state-funded compensatory programs was the Division of Compensatory Education, which already monitored federally funded Chapter 1 compensatory programs in over 90 percent of the districts in the state. Although the State Board of Education was scheduled to discuss whether to assign the responsibility of monitoring state compensatory education programs to the Division of Compensatory Education,[9] as of this writing this decision had not yet been made.

In the past, TEA's Division of State Funding was responsible for overseeing state compensatory education. However, this division was basically a "check-writing" agency responsible for ensuring that districts received their proper state aid allotments and exercised little oversight over how the allotments were spent. Given the small size of state compensatory education allotments before House Bill 72 and the loose restrictions on expenditures of the money, the division did not feel that monitoring districts' state compensatory education programs would be worth the expense.[10] Consequently, the only monitoring activity the Division of State Funding conducted in 1984-85 was to collect districts' one-page reports on how they spent their SCE funds.

State compensatory education has never been separately examined in the visits by TEA's Accreditation Division. These visits monitor a district's overall academic program and therefore may observe a compensatory class by chance, but they do not examine compensatory programs specifically. As a result, there is no real monitoring of the state compensatory education program.

House Bill 72 included a new provision which requires that districts report annually how they spend their state compensatory education allotment in each individual school. This information is to become part of each district's "performance report," in which the districts also report their students' average achievement test scores. In theory, this report could be the basis for monitoring SCE funds more closely, although written reports without on-site visits and enforcement provisions might not be very informative. As of this writing, however, TEA had not yet determined what specific information about district compensatory programs the performance reports would contain.

House Bill 72 enacted five new requirements indirectly related to compensatory education. The first requires students to pass all sections of a competency test "in mathematics and English language arts" in either the eleventh or twelfth grade in order to receive a high school diploma. This compels districts to offer remedial instruction to any student who fails a section of this test. The second mandates that districts provide "a remedial program for any student whose achievement test score was below a standard established by the State Board of Education." The "achievement test" is the TEAMS test, and the State Board of Education is expected to set this standard in July 1985.[11] In addition, the law requires districts to provide tutorials for students earning a grade less than 70 in any of their courses; this comes on top of a requirement in House Bill 246 that districts provide remedial instruction to any student who fails to master the essential elements. Finally, House Bill 72 requires many districts to provide compensatory prekindergarten programs and summer preschool programs for children with limited English proficiency; while these new programs, described at greater length in chapter 8, are funded separately from SCE, they do represent forms of compensatory education that can receive SCE funds.

If these obligations in House Bill 246 and House Bill 72 are enforced, then districts face numerous, even overwhelming, demands on their SCE money, and the absence of a supplement-not-supplant rule for state compensatory education may be irrelevant. By the time districts pay for the different forms of state-required remediation, they are not likely to have any state compensatory money left and may then be forced to commit local resources to pay for the cost of the required programs.

During the 1984-85 school year, however, none of these requirements—except tutorials and remediation for students who fail the TABS test—had gone into effect. The State Board of Education had not yet adopted the required competency test for high school graduation or the cutoff scores on the TEAMS test. The required preschool summer program was scheduled to go into effect in the summer of 1985, and the prekindergarten program in the fall of 1985; some districts postponed planning for these programs in the hope that the legislature would repeal the requirement for these programs. In addition, the House Bill 246 requirement that districts provide remediation for students who fail to master the essential elements was scheduled to go into effect in September 1985. The additional reporting requirement for districts' state compensatory education funds had not been implemented, and the monitoring of districts' state compensatory funds had not begun to take place.

With so many provisions of House Bill 246 and House Bill 72 not yet implemented, Texas school districts are far from feeling the complete fiscal effect of these requirements. The additional money provided by House Bill 72 came immediately, but some costs of implementing the legislation will be felt in subsequent years, particularly beginning in the 1985-86 school year. With the state legislature reluctant to levy additional taxes to support the full cost of what the legislation requires, one possible consequence is that the funds for meeting these requirements will come from local revenues. One potential danger is a new version of an old story; some districts, particularly those with low property tax bases, will have greater difficulty carrying out legislative obligations, while better-endowed districts will have little trouble.

HOW DISTRICTS SPEND THEIR STATE COMPENSATORY MONEY

According to their state reports for the 1983-84 school year, the districts in our survey reported spending the bulk of their state compensatory education money prior to House Bill 72 for remedial programs in reading and mathematics. Most of the money was used to pay the salaries of teachers involved in remediation. Out of sixteen districts examined, four districts, including one with more than a $1 million allotment, reported spending 100 percent of their state compensatory allotment on teacher salaries. Districts appeared to have concentrated a large proportion, possibly more than half, of state compensatory funding in grades seven through twelve. (In contrast, most districts concentrated the bulk of their Chapter 1 program funding in the elementary grades.) Two districts reported specific methods by which they co-ordinated their state and federal compensatory education programs. One of these trained high school seniors to work as student teachers in Chapter 1 schools, and a second district hired teachers and aides with SCE funds to aid the same student population served by Chapter 1.

How did the new requirements and the more than sixfold increase in state compensatory education under House Bill 72 affect these spending patterns? Of eighteen districts interviewed, seventeen received an increase in state compensatory funds. The state compensatory education funds in one wealthy district were eliminated because SCE was incorporated into the general state foundation aid formula, and this district did not qualify for aid under that formula.

In the seventeen districts that had increased state compensatory education money, nearly every one reported using some of the increase to pay for tutorials, and most planned to use state compensatory education money to pay for state-required prekindergarten and preschool summer bilingual programs. In addition, many districts were using SCE to cover part or all of the cost of tutoring students who failed the TABS test. Since the announcement of the increase came late in the summer after most districts had already adopted their budgets, several districts had not yet decided (as of winter 1985) how they would spend the increase.

Apart from meeting House Bill 72's requirements, the districts in the survey spent much of their state compensatory money on remedial reading and mathematics and computer-assisted instruction, particularly at the junior high level. Five districts indicated that they planned to use part of the funding increase to pay for remedial summer school.

In addition, the majority of the districts with large Hispanic or Asian populations spent much or most of their state compensatory education allotment on English as a Second Language programs. The fact that districts felt compelled to use state compensatory education funds for this purpose indicates that state ESL funding (described in greater detail in chapter 5) is inadequate. In certain districts with large newly immigrant Hispanic populations, such as those in the Valley, operating ESL programs appeared to be the main use for state compensatory funds.

A final use for state compensatory education money appeared to be to replace local funds previously spent on remediation. Of the eighteen districts in the survey that received SCE funding, three reported that they were likely to use part of this year's increase to pay for remedial programs previously supported by local funds. Austin, a district not in our survey, planned to use the entire increase in state compensatory education to pay for remedial programs previously supported with local funds, using the replaced local funds for a teacher salary increase. In effect, Austin will use the increase in SCE funds to raise teacher salaries. One small district reported that it lacks "a real compensatory education program" and simply "uses [the SCE money] where it is needed."

In sum, most state compensatory education money appeared to be spent to augment the districts' ability to operate remedial programs, although there is some use of state money in certain districts to pay for programs that would have been supported locally in the absence of state money. However, districts were already feeling the impact of the new state requirements, and an increasing proportion of state compensatory money was being used to satisfy those requirements. In addition, districts with large immigrant populations were finding state compensatory education funding to be a useful substitute for inadequate state funding for bilingual and ESL instruction.

CONCLUSIONS AND RECOMMENDATIONS

Over the last thirty years, state aid in Texas has been viewed not as supplemental funds added to local revenues, but a subsidy to districts to provide a minimum level of expenditures which local spending may supplement. Consequently, the lack of interest in a requirement that state compensatory education supplement rather than supplant local compensatory education spending should not come as a surprise. However, the consequence of not having this requirement in the past was that the state had to provide a larger increase in SCE aid in order to make a difference in compensatory spending, because districts were likely to use part of the increase to pay for programs previously supported by local effort.

The enactment of new legislation requiring districts to operate extensive remedial programs has fundamentally changed this situation. Despite the significant increase in state compensatory funding, many districts have found SCE funding inadequate to carry out the remedial tasks mandated by the state. Since several state requirements--including preschool summer programs, prekindergarten programs, and remediation for students falling below state standards on the TEAMS test or failing to master essential elements--have not yet taken effect, many school district administrators may soon discover that their SCE funds are insufficient, despite the increases in House Bill 72.

Another large question that remains is how to make state-funded compensatory programs more effective. One possible approach, followed by a number of other states in their compensatory education programs, is to make state compensatory aid more like Chapter 1: to institute more formal procedures for determining which children are to be served, to evaluate whether programs are successful, and to determine whether programs supplement a required minimum level of local effort. This approach poses the familiar dilemma of state versus local control and is not likely to be popular with districts which want flexibility to use state compensatory education funds to benefit any student who needs remediation, whether that student is educationally disadvantaged or not.

A more promising approach would be to strengthen the role of the Texas Education Agency in providing technical assistance to districts to improve their SCE-funded programs. Such a strategy could consist of two parts. The first could be a mandate, passed by the legislature and backed by appropriate funding, that TEA provide technical assistance to districts in evaluating and improving their SCE-funded programs. As part of this program, the Education Service Centers could train school district personnel to use test scores and other evaluation results to improve their SCE-funded programs, just as now happens with federal compensatory education. The second element could be a system to discover successful state compensatory education programs and disseminate their methods throughout the state.

Clearly, the Texas legislature made a substantial commitment to compensatory education in House Bill 72, most obviously in a sizable expansion of funds. To make sure these dollars are spent wisely, the state could spend a few extra cents to evaluate and improve the quality of these programs.

Notes

[1]Benjamin Stickney and Virginia Plunkett, "Closing the Gap: A Historical Perspective on the Effectiveness of Compensatory Education," Phi Delta Kappan 65 (December 1983): 287-90.

[2]Launor Carter, A Study of Compensatory and Elementary Education: The Sustaining Effects Study, Final Report (System Development Corporation for the U.S. Department of Education, January 1983).

[3]Because the adjusted basic allotment in 1984-85 equaled $1,290 x (1 + .75(PDI-1)), the value of the SCE allocation was influenced by the PDI. For districts with the maximum PDI of 1.282, for example, the adjusted basic allotment was $1,563, and the extra funds for state compensatory education equaled $313 per low-income child.

[4]Education Consolidation and Improvement Act of 1981, 20 U.S.C. Annotated 3805, PL 97-35 as amended by PL 98-211 (November 1983).

[5]Telephone interview with Paul Mettke, Assistant Director, Texas Education Agency Division of Compensatory Education, Austin, Texas, April 25, 1985. At the time of the interview, twenty of the twenty-three positions were filled, and the agency was seeking applicants for the other three positions.

[6]Telephone interview with an employee in the Texas Education Agency Division of Accreditation, Austin, Texas, March 19, 1985.

[7]Education Consolidation and Improvement Act of 1981, 20 U.S.C. 3805, Sec. 556(e).

[8]Texas Education Code, Sec. 16.176(f).

[9]Telephone interview with Jim Wilson, Director, Division of Compensatory Education, Texas Education Agency, Austin, Texas, March 19, 1985.

[10]Telephone interview with Tom Patton, Director, Division of State Funding, Texas Education Agency, Austin, Texas, February 21, 1985.

[11]Interview with Dave Jones, Researcher, Division of Educational Assessment, Texas Education Agency, Austin, Texas, March 22, 1985. In addition, the TEAMS test is to be administered in the first and seventh grades as well as the third, fifth, and ninth grades as was required previously. TEAMS is a revision of the Texas Assessment of Basic Skills test.

CHAPTER FIVE
CHANGES IN STATE-FUNDED BILINGUAL EDUCATION

Like compensatory education, bilingual education is a program for a group of children--those of limited English proficiency, or LEP--to enhance their education. As in the case of compensatory education, most of the early developments in bilingual education came from the federal government. A small state-funded program was substantially increased by House Bill 72, providing opportunities to expand bilingual programs. Unfortunately, this expansion has coincided with other problems that bilingual education faces: a decline in federal support; an increased LEP population in Texas schools, because of immigration from Mexico, Central America, and the Orient; and shortages of certified bilingual teachers. One important question is whether increases in state funding are adequate to address these problems or whether bilingual programs will fall behind despite the changes of House Bill 72.

EARLY FEDERAL DEVELOPMENTS

The history of bilingual education has been closely associated with the increase of Hispanics in the United States, currently estimated to be the fastest-growing minority group in the United States and 21 percent of the population in Texas.[1] Most studies of Mexican American students in the 1960s concluded that four factors hindered their economic and educational development: they do badly in school, drop out early, are poor, and speak primarily Spanish.[2] The National Commission on Employment Policy concluded that limited English proficiency was the crucial problem for Mexican Americans and that, of various barriers to success in the American job market, "by far the most important is difficulty with English."[3] Since language barriers lead both to poor school performance and to underemployment in labor markets, the need to reduce limited English proficiency from an early age was obvious.

In the early 1960s, however, there was some question about the effectiveness of bilingual education for students of Limited English Speaking Ability (LESA). Results from early bilingual studies viewed bilingualism as detrimental to intellectual functioning and success in school. Bilingual education came to be viewed more positively only after a comprehensive study in 1962 of six French schools in Montreal. The results showed that "bilinguals perform significantly better than monolinguals on both verbal and nonverbal intelligence tests. . . the bilinguals appear to have a more diversified set of mental abilities than the monolinguals."[4] The late sixties brought an increase in public support and discussion of bilingual education. The National Advisory Committee on Mexican American Education addressed the problem of limited English proficiency. The committee recommended that instruction be conducted in both English and Spanish and that teachers be better prepared in instructing bilingual education. As Father Henry J. Casso proclaimed during a conference on Mexican American education, "Ya Basta, The Siesta Is Over!"[5]

For the first time, Congress addressed the need with the passage of the Bilingual Education Act of 1968. The act established an advisory committee on bilingual education and developed a mechanism for federal funding of programs.[6] The act provided that the "highest priority" be given districts with large numbers of children from non-English-speaking backgrounds and also furnished funds for teacher education in bilingual techniques.[7] However, funding remained meager.

In 1970, the Department of Health, Education, and Welfare (HEW) directed districts with LESA student populations of 5 percent or greater to provide special language programs, based on the Civil Rights Act of 1964,[8] forbidding discrimination in education based on race, color, religion, or national origin. These directives were challenged in court and upheld in a 1974 opinion which significantly changed the future course of bilingual education. In the case of Lau v. Nichols, 414 U.S. 563, the Supreme Court ruled that the San Francisco Unified School District was not in compliance with the Civil Rights Act of 1964.[9] The Court asserted, "we know that those who do not understand English are certain to find their classroom experiences wholly incomprehensible and in no way meaningful" and went on to state that the plaintiffs, a group of non-English-speaking Chinese students, were discriminated against when the classroom and instruction techniques ignored their lack of English proficiency.[10] The justices ruled that special programs were necessary. In 1975, HEW developed a set of guidelines to interpret the Supreme Court ruling, known as the Lau remedies. These are outlines of alternative solutions and programs for bilingual education, and were initially used to mandate bilingual programs in over five hundred school districts across the nation.

BILINGUAL METHODS AND THEIR EFFECTIVENESS

Various programs exist today that help LEP students in their efforts to comprehend and speak English: submersion; English as a Second Language; immersion; transitional bilingual education (TBE); and bilingual-bicultural programs.

1. Submersion: LEP students are placed in regular classrooms where only English is spoken. Submersion is aptly called the "sink or swim" approach to language deficiencies. The LEP student's home language is not spoken at all in the classroom, and no attempt is made to retain the student's native language and culture. Submersion is not properly considered a bilingual method, of course.

2. English as a Second Language: Ideally, teachers use ESL as a component of a complete bilingual curriculum. However, it is most widely used today as the sole instructional technique for LEP children. Typically, ESL instruction takes place in English during one class period; for the rest of the day ESL students are placed in regular classrooms (in other words, in submersion).

3. Immersion: Immersion instruction is in English, as is ESL, but

immersion teaches subject matter and English simultaneously, and the student's native language is therefore used in a variety of classes. Vocabulary is introduced slowly as the subject matter requires.

4. Transitional Bilingual Education: TBE teaches reading in both the LEP student's home language and English. The subject matter is taught in the home language until the student's English proficiency allows the student to attend regular classes.

5. Bilingual-Bicultural: Bilingual-bicultural education is similar to the TBE program, but the bilingual-bicultural approach emphasizes the importance of teaching the student's native culture and language throughout the elementary and secondary years.[11]

There are shortcomings and problems with each of these models. The transitional bilingual technique ignores the value of retaining bilingualism in the child, since the bilingual-bicultural curriculum is abandoned once the pupil achieves fluency in English. ESL does not incorporate cultural or bilingual aspects into its program, and many consider it merely a supplement to the other models. Immersion has proven effective among French Canadian students, but it is not effective among Hispanics. Middle to upper class status--an advantage most Hispanics don't enjoy--plays important roles in the success of the Canadian experiment in immersion.[12]

Not surprisingly, there have been vociferous critics of any form of bilingualism. Opponents feel that bilingual education fosters ethnic separatism and fails to provide English proficiency as rapidly as immersion programs.[13]

The Department of Education found that some bilingual instructional techniques actually harmed the educational development of students.[14] The negative effects of bilingual programs were attributed to poor techniques of assessing need. A student is classified as LEP if he or she performs below a certain level of English proficiency and comes from a non-English speaking background. However, many students who performed worse in a bilingual program were less proficient in their home language than in English; therefore, bilingual methods presented additional barriers rather than help in improving their English.

There is little doubt, however, that the majority of special language programs are effective in improving the educational performance of the LEP students.[15] Furthermore, a recent study refutes the claim that bilingual programs stall the integration of minority groups into American society. The study found instead that special language programs result in greater parental involvement in schools and community and that parents became "more integrated into the educational and political system on local, state, and national levels when their children were enrolled in bilingual programs."[16] In sum, the research shows that bilingual education is often a more effective instructional method for the LEP child, although there is still some uncertainty about which of the four bilingual instructional methods is most effective.

CURRENT NATIONAL ISSUES

The dominant national issue in bilingual education over the past few years has been the effort of the Reagan Administration to reduce federal spending on education as part of the attempt to cut spending on special programs. Since 1980, there has been a 46 percent reduction in federal bilingual funds;[17] as a result, only half of the school districts applying for federal bilingual funds are currently receiving them.[18] The Administration has also rescinded proposed regulations concerning state compliance.[19] Regulations are necessary, however, because Title VII of the Bilingual Education Act of 1968 does not obligate school districts to provide bilingual education, but merely provides supplemental funds for districts that want them. The Lau decision mandates the implementation of a special language program, but it does not specify what type of program should be used. Furthermore, the Lau remedies specify preferred instructional techniques, but they are not legally enforceable.[20] As a result, federal regulations are necessary to ensure that districts implement comprehensive and appropriate bilingual programs in districts that need them.[21] Many supporters of bilingual education fear that school districts are doing just enough to comply with federal regulations, so that weaker federal regulations will hamper efforts to develop more comprehensive programs.

Finally, the Reagan Administration has attempted to reverse the gains made by bilingual supporters. It has asserted that local school districts, rather than the federal government, should be responsible for developing programs for non-English-speaking students--despite the fact that few local districts provided any bilingual education prior to federal funding. Furthermore, the Reagan Administration supports ESL rather than native language development and time limits on federal funding in order to encourage eventual funding solely at the local level;[22] as a result, the Administration originally proposed that bilingual education programs be cut 72 percent from $180 million to $50 million.[23] Only heavy lobbying by the bilingual education community prevented such a serious reduction.

These attacks on bilingual education come at a time when many bilingual educators and administrators believe essential improvements are needed, including more bilingual education programs for teachers, continuing bilingual education in high school and college, and development of community activities for bilingual adults who are out of school.[24] Furthermore, they come at a time when Texas has experienced an increase in its bilingual populations, including both Spanish-speaking children and Oriental children.

BILINGUAL EDUCATION IN TEXAS

The initial legislation requiring bilingual education in the elementary grade was passed by the 1973 legislature, but enrollments were relatively low.[25] In 1975, the Office of Civil Rights of the Department of Health, Education, and Welfare identified 59 school districts in Texas out of 300 nationally that would be required to institute special language programs for LESA students.[26] In 1981, Texas passed legislation (S.B. 477) containing specific requirements for bilingual education in school districts where the need existed.[27] These requirements include the following:

1. If a district identifies twenty or more LEP students at any grade level for a given language, the district is required to offer bilingual instruction (as opposed to ESL) for grades K-5 in that language.

2. If a district identifies between one and twenty LEP students at a grade level for a given language, the district must provide one 45-minute period of ESL instruction per day.

3. At the secondary level all LEP students must be provided with at least forty-five minutes of ESL instruction per day.   Bilingual programs at the secondary level are voluntary.[28]

4. Texas is one of thirteen states requiring bilingual teacher certification.[29]

These state standards are stricter than the federal bilingual requirements, which stipulate special language instruction for LEP students but do not specify a particular educational technique, set class size, or provide for teacher certification. As a result, all Texas school districts meeting the regulations of S.B. 477 are considered in compliance with federal guidelines.

All federal funds for bilingual education are to be used as supplements to local and state special language funding; this requirement is equivalent to the supplement-not-supplant rule in federal compensatory education. Federal bilingual funds come from a variety of sources, such as migrant education grants, Chapter 1 (compensatory education), and Chapter 2 (the Education Block Grant). However, the majority of federal funding comes from Title VII authorizations.   Local districts must apply for these funds directly through the Department of Education.   Each district must submit a copy of its application to TEA for review and comment, and the agency also has the authority to enforce compliance and with federal requirements.

CHANGES IN STATE BILINGUAL FUNDING

Prior to House Bill 72, bilingual programs in Texas were funded through a foundation grant. The state provided local districts with $12.50 per LEP student in an ESL program and $50 per LEP student in a bilingual program. The total state funding from the grant was $9.7 million in 1983-84.[30] Under this funding structure, 25 percent of the funding received by local districts was required to be spent on teacher training. The other 75 percent could be spent on programs and on pupil evaluation, instructional materials, and supplemental staff expenses, including salaries.

House Bill 72 changed state funding for bilingual education. The bill transformed the previous grants of $12.50 and $50 per pupil for ESL and bilingual education into a weighted pupil formula similar to that for compensatory education. The new House Bill 72 funding formula calls for allocation of the adjusted basic allotment ($1,290) multiplied by (.1) for every student in a special language program, for a minimum supplement of $129 per pupil.[31] The allotment is the same for students enrolled in bilingual and ESL programs. The funding change resulted in an increase in state funding from $9.7 million to $35 million for bilingual education.[32] The 25 percent previously allocated for staff development is no longer required. In its place, the State Board allows districts to use up to 15 percent of bilingual funds for general administrative costs.

On the surface, the considerable increase in funding appears to be a victory for bilingual supporters and LEP students, and the districts we interviewed welcomed the increased funding. However, many questioned whether the new funding mechanism would solve the difficulties facing bilingual education in Texas, because House Bill 72 comes at a time when other problems are increasing and other sources of funds are dwindling.

One problem is that total spending on bilingual programs from state, federal, and local sources will not increase in some school districts, for several reasons. Some districts reported that they were already experiencing a decrease in local funds for bilingual programs. Consequently, they will use the increased state dollars to compensate for the loss of local monies.[33] In addition, other changes in House Bill 72, such as maximum class size of twenty-two students and tutorial programs, will require additional local funds; therefore, the increased bilingual funding may be used to supplant local dollars which were previously spent on bilingual projects. State funds are not required to supplement current programs and supplanting of local funds by state bilingual money can be achieved under the auspices of "general administrative costs" allowed under House Bill 72.

Finally, since 1978, there has been a significant decrease in federal Title VII money granted to Texas schools. In 1978, the state was receiving $21 million; today, that figure has dropped to $6 million. Oscar Cardenas, director of the Division of Bilingual Education of the Texas Education Agency, attributes the decline in Title VII funds not only to reduced appropriations, but also to intimidating audits conducted by the U.S. Department of Education in 1981, which made some local districts reluctant to apply for federal funds for fear of future audits.[34] During January to August 1981, the Office of the Inspector General for Audit of the Department of Education conducted a review of seventeen Title VII projects. It concluded that Title VII funding in Texas had little impact on bilingual education and requested that the Department of Education terminate several projects and refund approximately $6 million in misused funds to the federal government. (Later, the Office of the Inspector General reduced this claim to $66,000 after an appeals process.)[35] Increased state bilingual funds will, in essence, be replacing Title VII money in some districts and thus not substantially supplementing existing programs.

Another potential problem with the House Bill 72 bilingual provisions is the elimination of the requirement that districts spend 25 percent of state bilingual funds on staff development. This change, which allows districts more freedom, may have some positive effects. For example, many districts are using the increased funding on salary increases as well as staff development, to attempt to reduce chronic bilingual and ESL teacher shortages. However, the elimination of staff development requirements is occurring at a time when there is a serious shortage of bilingual teachers and an increasing number of bilingual and ESL teachers are uncertified and underqualified. Without a requirement for staff development, districts are not required to aid teachers in acquiring bilingual or ESL teaching credentials.

A final concern about the new bilingual funding is that many districts with large LEP populations spend a high percentage of their state compensatory education money, in addition to state and federal bilingual funds, on ESL and bilingual programs. The fact that districts must use this SCE money to supplement state bilingual funds indicates that bilingual funding is still insufficient, despite the increases in House Bill 72.

THE NEVER-ENDING PROBLEM: SHORTAGES OF BILINGUAL TEACHERS

The most serious problem facing bilingual education in Texas and the nation is the shortage of qualified bilingual teachers.[36] The proliferation of monolingual, uncertified teachers in ESL and bilingual classrooms is a by-product of this shortage. In 1982, only two states reported that their supply of bilingual teachers was adequate, while forty states indicated that their supply was inadequate.[37] In Texas, most of the district officials we interviewed expressed concern over bilingual teacher shortages. One measure of the shortage is that in 1984-85, thirty-one districts--16 percent of those required to provide bilingual education--applied for waivers from TEA because of these shortages.

One factor contributing to the shortage of bilingual teachers in Texas was a 2 percent increase in LEP students in 1984. These increases in the LEP population were due not only to an influx of immigrants from Asia, Cuba, and Central America, but also to improved LEP identification procedures. TEA has recently found significant departures from state law when districts fail to identify LEP students enrolled in the regular curriculum,[38] and measures to improve LEP identification will continue to increase the numbers of LEP students and thus the shortage of bilingual teachers. Second, between 1974 and 1978, many underqualified and uncertified bilingual teachers were given official certification through a grandfather clause passed by the Texas legislature.[39] In 1981-82, ESL teachers were exempted from the new certification requirements if they continued to teach in their district, and TEA admits a significant number of teachers were grandfathered under this provision.[40] Another factor affecting bilingual teacher shortages is that many qualified bilingual teachers are not teaching in bilingual classrooms. Many bilingual graduates from education schools seek regular classroom and administrative positions.[41] Some bilingual teachers accept positions in the private sector because the pay scale for bilingual teachers does not compensate for the extra work required of them.[42]

A further problem for bilingual education is that colleges and universities are not graduating a sufficient number of bilingual teachers. For all disciplines, the number of Texas education school graduates peaked in 1973-74 at 16,000. By 1980-81, there were only 12,000 graduates.[43] The general decline in education school graduates has affected bilingual graduates especially: in 1983-84 there were only 303 graduates of Texas education schools certified in bilingual education or ESL.[44] As a result, many districts are forced to recruit bilingual teachers from other states. Some educators feel that their recruits often do not understand the cultural complexities of Texas communities very well.

Several provisions of House Bill 72 are likely to exacerbate the shortage of bilingual teachers. The new maximum class size of twenty-two pupils in kindergarten through grade two will require more elementary classroom teachers; in some areas, particularly in the Valley, this will draw some bilingual teachers out of bilingual programs. The summer bilingual preschool programs will also require the hiring of bilingual teachers, although this will presumably not reduce the numbers teaching during the regular school year. The prospect of minimum competency testing of teachers also complicates the shortage. First, many uncertified teachers currently teaching on waivers might fail an exam testing their Spanish language skills. Second, many bilingual instructors in Texas are Hispanic, and results from Arizona show that a larger percentage of minorities fail minimum competency exams than do Anglos,[45] an outcome often attributed to cultural biases in the exams. A competency exam may therefore result in fewer bilingual teachers because of failure or refusal to take the exam.

Finally, some districts feel that the equalization effects of House Bill 72 will result in better salaries paid to teachers in the Rio Grande Valley, where there are a large number of qualified bilingual instructors. In turn, other areas of the state with bilingual teacher shortages may find it more difficult to lure teachers from the Valley schools.

CONCLUSIONS AND RECOMMENDATIONS

Despite the substantial increases in state funding for bilingual education, decreases in local and federal funds and increases in numbers of LEP students have partially offset the potential benefit of House Bill 72. In particular, the provisions of House Bill 72 did not directly address the serious shortages of bilingual teachers, and some requirements of the bill even may make these shortages worse. Until the chronic undersupply of qualified bilingual teachers can be reduced, other issues in bilingual education--especially the efforts to improve programs and to determine which of the different models of bilingual education work best under what conditions--must be postponed.

A variety of possible solutions can be developed to help reduce bilingual teacher shortages. Incentive pay plans have been successful in some local districts. In 1978-79, the Houston Independent School District adopted a program called the Second Mile Plan to help reduce teacher shortages in critical fields, including bilingual education. The program provides a $1,500 pay incentive in the hope of attracting qualified bilingual teachers. As a result, the proportion of teachers who resigned, took a leave, retired, or transferred decreased from 23.9 percent in 1978-79 to 16.9 percent in the 1983-84 school year, and the number of teacher vacancies for all fields decreased from 613 in August 1979 to 120 in August 1983. These improvements all took place while Texas was experiencing an increase in teacher shortages in math, science, and special language instruction. However, local funding is essential to a comprehensive incentive program. In Houston alone, the first four years of implementing the Second Mile Plan have cost $27.9 million.[46]

Coordination with local community colleges should also be sought as a means to reduce shortages. Local districts can hire qualified bilingual teachers in community colleges to teach part-time at area high schools.[47] However, this solution is limited to districts with community colleges nearby.

Teacher loans could be reinstituted to reduce chronic shortages. In 1958, through the National Defense Education Act (NDEA), Congress gave low interest loans for math, science, and foreign language students entering teaching. Each year a teacher taught in an area of need, 10 percent of the loan was forgiven, to a maximum of five years.[48] The loans made under the NDEA were effective in the past and could be tried again. The teacher loan program included in House Bill 72 is a step in this direction, although most educators feel that it is insufficient to increase the supply of teachers substantially.

Texas could also adopt policies that assist the movement of bilingual teachers from areas of adequate supply (such as the Valley) to areas of low supply. Policies like portable pensions, interstate reciprocity of teacher credentials and competency tests, and transfer of credit for years of experience between state districts will aid in the movement of teachers to districts of low supply.[49]

Furthermore, in-service staff development can be implemented through the use of state funds to retrain teachers from surplus areas such as history and social studies and place them in bilingual programs.[50] The inadequate certification of many Texas bilingual and ESL teachers indicates that not enough is being done in the area of staff development.

Other regions of the United States experiencing bilingual teacher shortages are effectively addressing the problem by coordinating college and district efforts. For example, between 1978 and 1984, the Chicago area developed a program at the University of Illinois at Chicago to address the city's bilingual teacher shortage. The Chicago program formed a linkage between the university and the community bilingual teachers and officials in order to assess the local district's needs accurately. The college emphasized the instruction of students in the uses of English and Spanish in all areas, including math and science. The program also developed a new career path in education for Hispanic Americans and other qualified speakers who might not otherwise consider teaching as a profession. Other ideas included using bilingual teachers in the Chicago schools to act as paid consultants to conduct workshops at the university level.[51] Such efforts could be adopted in Texas, where the state's colleges and universities are clearly not preparing enough bilingual teachers.

Notes

[1]Sister Marie Andre Walsh, The Development of a Rationale for a Program to Prepare Teachers for Spanish Speaking Children in the Bilingual-Bicultural Elementary School (San Francisco: R and E Research Associates, 1976), 3.

[2]Thomas P. Carter, Mexican Americans in School: A History of Educational Neglect (New York: College Entrance Examination Board, 1970), 3.

[3]National Commission on Employment Policy, Hispanics and Jobs: Barriers to Progress (Washington, D.C.: U.S. Government Printing Office, 1982), 1.

[4]Carter, Mexican Americans in School, 49-50.

[5]Father Henry J. Casso, "Ya Basta, The Siesta Is Over," in Educating the Mexican American, ed. Henry Sioux Johnson and William J. Hernandez-M. (Valley Forge, Penn.: Judson, 1970), 97-98.

[6]National Commission on Employment Policy, Hispanics and Jobs, 85.

[7]Congressional Quarterly Weekly Report 25 (December 1967): 2617.

[8]Charles R. Foster, "Defusing the Issues in Bilingualism and Bicultural Education," Phi Delta Kappan 63 (January 1982): 342.

[9]National Commission on Employment Policy, Hispanics and Jobs, 85.

[10]Arnold H. Leibowitz, Federal Recognition of the Rights of Minority Language Groups (Rosslyn, Va.: National Clearinghouse for Bilingual Education, 1982), 132.

[11]Keith A. Baker and Adrianna A. de Kanter, "An Answer from Research on Bilingual Education," American Education 19 (July 1983): 40.

[12]David P. Baral, "Second Language Acquisition Theories Relevant to Bilingual Education," in Theory Technology and Public Policy on Bilingual Education, ed. Raymond V. Padilla (Rosslyn, Va.: National Clearinghouse for Bilingual Education, 1983), 10.

[13]U. S. Commission on Civil Rights, A Better Chance to Learn: Bilingual Bicultural Education, Publication no. 51 (Washington, D.C.: U.S. Government Printing Office, May 1985): 13

[14]Baker and de Kanter, "An Answer," 46.

[15]Ibid.

[16]Dr. Gloria Zamora, President of the National Association for Bilingual Education, speaking before the House Subcommittee on Census and Population, Bilingual Journal 7, no. 4 (Summer 1983): 6.

[17]U.S. Commission on Civil Rights, Statement on the Fiscal Year 1984 Education Budget (Washington, D.C.: U.S. Commission on Civil Rights Clearinghouse, July 1983), 16.

[18]Civil Rights Leadership Conference Fund, An Oath Betrayed: The Reagan Administration's Civil Rights Enforcement Record in Education (Washington, D.C.: Civil Rights Leadership Conference Fund, 1983).

[19]Muhammad A. Shuraydi, "Bilingual Bicultural Education: A Humanistic Multiethnic Challenge," in Theory, Technology, and Public Policy On Bilingual Education, ed. Raymond V. Padilla (Rosslyn, Va.: National Clearinghouse for Bilingual Education, 1983), 395-96.

[20]Baker and de Kanter, "An Answer," 41.

[21]Civil Rights Leadership Conference Fund, An Oath Betrayed, 36-37.

[22]"News," Bilingual Journal 8 (Fall 1983-Winter 1984): 4.

[23]Telephone interview with Sam Saenz, Public Information Officer, U.S. Department of Education, Regional Office, Dallas, Texas, October 18, 1984.

[24]Guadalupe Valdes, "Planning for Biliteracy," in Spanish In the U.S. Setting and beyond the Southwest, ed. Lucia Elias-Olivares (Rosslyn, Va.: National Clearinghouse for Bilingual Education, 1983), 259.

[25]"Application for Coordination of Technical Assistance in Bilingual Education by Texas Education Agency, 1983-84," Division of Bilingual Education, Texas Education Agency, undated.

[26]Telephone interview with Oscar Cardenas, Director of the Division of Bilingual Education, Texas Education Agency, Austin, Texas, February 19, 1985.

[27]Kris T. Rugssaken, "Toward True Bilingual Education: When Federal Funding Ends," Bilingual Journal 29 (Summer 1983): 11.

[28]Telephone interview with Elisa Gutierrez, Division of Bilingual Education, Texas Education Agency, Austin, Texas, October 26, 1984.

[29]Rugssaken, "Toward True Bilingual Education," 11.

[30]Interview with Oscar Cardenas, February 19, 1985.

[31]As in state compensatory education, this supplement increases with PDI and equals $157 for districts with the highest PDI of 1.289 supplement per bilingual pupil.

[32]Interview with Oscar Cardenas, February 19, 1985.

[33]Interview with Delia Pampa, Executive Director, Bilingual Department, and Rose Hicks, Deputy Supervisor of Special Programs, Houston Independent School District, Houston, Texas, December 6, 1984.

[34]Interview with Oscar Cardenas, October 11, 1984.

[35]The districts that had been audited and TEA challenged the findings of the Office of the Inspector General and requested an oversight hearing before the Subcommittee on Education and Labor of the U.S. Congress. The hearing, convened in July 1983, concluded that the Office of the Inspector General had overstepped its authority. On appeal, the claim of $5.8 million in misused funds was reduced to $66,000. However, the report of the Inspector General had already alleged that waste, fraud, and abuse was widespread in bilingual programs, presenting a negative image of bilingual education. Many bilingual educators feel that the Office of the Inspector General was on a witchhunt attempting to discredit unfairly bilingual education. Letter from Oscar Cardenas, Division of Bilingual Education, TEA, July 11, 1985.

[36]Alan Pifer, "Bilingual Education and the Hispanic Challenge," Education Digest 46 (November 1980): 12-15; Rugssaken, "Toward True Bilingual Education," 9.

[37]Kenneth Nickel, "Bilingual Education in the Eighties," Phi Delta Kappan 63 (May 1982): 638.

[38]Interview with Oscar Cardenas, February 19, 1985.

[39]Interview with Robert Tipton, Education Specialist II, Division of Bilingual Education, Texas Education Agency, Austin, Texas, March 18, 1985.

[40]Interview with Oscar Cardenas, February 19, 1985.

[41]Interview with Sam Saenz, October 18, 1984; telephone interview with Gloria Contreras, Professor of Education, The University of Texas at Austin, Austin, Texas, October 16, 1984.

[42]Telephone interview with John O'Sullivan, Treasurer, Texas Federation of Teachers, Austin, Texas, October 16, 1984.

[43]Clifton S. Harris, "The Responses of Teacher Educators to the Shortage of Teachers in Texas," Phi Delta Kappan 64 (December 1982): 287.

[44]Interview with Robert Tipton, March 18, 1985.

[45]Arnold M. Gallegos, "The Negative Consequences of Teacher Competency Testing," Phi Delta Kappan 65 (May 1984): 631.

[46]Houston Independent School District, The Second Mile Plan, Houston, Texas, 1984.

[47]James W. Guthrie and Ami Zusman, "Teacher Supply and Demand in Mathematics and Science," Phi Delta Kappan 64 (September 1982): 30-33.

[48]Ibid.

[49]Charles T. Kenchner, "Shortages and Gluts of Public School Teachers: There Must Be a Policy Problem Somewhere," Public Administration Review 44 (July/August 1984): 292-98.

[50]Guthrie and Zusman, "Teacher Supply and Demand," 30.

[51]Lisa Baldonado, "A University Program to Meet Chicago's Bilingual Needs," Bilingual Journal 7 (Summer 1983): 15-17.

CHAPTER SIX
STATE-SUPPORTED SPECIAL EDUCATION FOR HANDICAPPED CHILDREN

Like compensatory and bilingual education, special programs for handicapped children are a legacy of movements to provide greater educational opportunities to students whose needs had been neglected by the schools. In the case of handicapped students, this neglect was often complete, since many handicapped pupils in the past have been effectively barred from public education. As for compensatory and bilingual education, national developments and federal programs led in the development of education for the handicapped. But state efforts have increased as well, and House Bill 72 provides a new funding mechanism and increased funding for special education. However, unlike the case of compensatory education (where federal requirements are stringent and state requirements nonexistent) and bilingual education (where state requirements are more stringent than federal regulation), there are possibilities for serious conflict between state financing for special education and federal regulations.

THE ANTECEDENTS OF EDUCATION FOR THE HANDICAPPED

Publicly supported education for the handicapped has had a long and uneven history in the United States. Since the 1830s, state-supported institutions have existed to provide education and training to disabled individuals.[1] These institutions were generally statewide schools for people with particular handicaps, such as state schools for the blind. Toward the end of the century, many states introduced special classes within the regular school system, but education for the handicapped was still inconsistent and irregular.

Prior to the Second World War, the courts were rather unsympathetic to the educational rights of the handicapped. In 1917, for example, a Wisconsin judge ruled in the Beattie case that disabled children could be denied admission to a public school if their presence had a "depressing and nauseating effect on the teachers and school children,"[2] and this attitude was typical of other states.

However, negative attitudes toward the handicapped had changed considerably by the 1970s. Various court decisions at the state level upheld the rights of disabled children to receive a public education. Two cases, Mills v. Pennsylvania and Mills v. Board of Education of the District of Columbia, both decided in 1972, had a profound effect on establishing this right. By 1974, all fifty states had legislated some form of special education programs.[3]

Prior to these cases, federal involvement under the Handicapped Act and the Elementary and Secondary Education Act, both of 1965, was limited to funding for research and technical assistance to state authorities establishing special education programs. By 1974, on the crest of movements that established the federal government's role in civil rights and education,

Congress considered direct funding for special education for the first time. In that year, the Handicapped Act was amended to provide some financial assistance. However, the most important piece of legislation dealing with special education in American history came the following year.

The Education for All Handicapped Children Act of 1975, PL 94-142, has been the main focus of educational policy for the disabled during the last decade. The law's stated intent is to assure a "free and appropriate public education" for all handicapped children.[4] At the time of the act's passage, only 59 percent of the country's handicapped were served in public school systems.[5] PL 94-142 established requirements governing how school districts must treat handicapped children and their parents. The law requires that, in order to receive federal funds, each local education agency (LEA) must oversee a proper program for special education and draw up annual plans for achieving the goal of full educational opportunity. LEAs also must keep extensive records of the process by which they formulate Individual Education Plans (IEPs) for each student. Parents are supposed to play an active role throughout this process. To support the requirements of PL 94-142, funds are allocated to each state based on the estimated number of handicapped students between the ages of three and twenty-one. PL 94-142 funds are restricted to use in special education, and school districts may not use the funds to supplant local funds until all the disabled students in the districts are served. State education agencies are responsible for implementation of PL 94-142 requirements, including monitoring and analyzing LEA activities.

One of the most important provisions in PL 94-142 was the requirement that all students in special education must be put in the "least restrictive educational" environment possible. This process, known as mainstreaming, assumes that handicapped students should be integrated with their peers in regular educational situations as much as possible. Much of the philosophy behind mainstreaming was similar to the reasoning in earlier racial desegregation cases like Brown v. Board of Education; it was deemed an infraction of handicapped children's rights to segregate them unnecessarily from the other children. Mainstreaming also gained support from research conducted in the 1960s and 1970s which suggested that, in many cases, combined classes enhance the academic achievement of handicapped children.[6] To be sure, mainstreaming has been a radical departure from days past, when handicapped children were usually placed in separate classrooms (if not separate schools), and mainstreaming was resisted in the beginning. Many educators feared that having to deal with the special needs of a disabled student would take time away from instruction of the children. Nonetheless, mainstreaming has become generally accepted as part of the professional ideal of a proper special education program, though there remain debates about the mainstreaming of more profoundly handicapped children.

The most serious controversy that arose over PL 94-142 involved the financial burden that the act placed on states and localities. On the whole, PL 94-142 greatly increased the level of service that LEAs had to provide without providing sufficient federal aid to cover these costs, and both states and local education agencies were forced to increase their funding levels. This has resulted in constant skirmishing over the funding of special education, with litigation against school districts necessary to force them to comply with PL 94-142. The requirements of PL94-142 often affect poorer school districts more adversely than others, because greater numbers of handicapped children generally reside in them. These districts usually had less well developed special education programs to begin with.[7]

Unlike the cases of compensatory education and bilingual education, federal funds for handicapped children have not been cut during the Reagan Administration, so districts and states have not been forced to increase their own revenues to compensate for declining federal funds. However, under Reagan, the U.S. Department of Education has relaxed some regulations.[8] This has had the effect of weakening the provisions of PL 94-142 because of the importance of such regulations (as distinct from federal funding) in forcing districts to comply.

STATE SUPPORT FOR SPECIAL EDUCATION IN TEXAS

Texas has had a respectable record so far in the area of special education. The 1969 legislature passed Senate Bill 230, the Comprehensive Special Education Act. This act was intended to provide educational services for handicapped children in a "coordinated and integrated manner. Between 1969 and 1978, during which PL 94-142 came into effect, the percentage of all students in average daily attendance served by special education programs increased from 5.6 percent to 13.1 percent."[9]

House Bill 72 revised the method of funding state-supported special education, in order to provide varying levels of funding for programs based on the costs of different types of instructional activities. In place of a system that funded programs at large on a personnel unit basis, House Bill 72 established a system of weights for each type of instructional arrangement, similar to the weights of 1.2 and 1.1 for children in compensatory education and bilingual education but quite different in magnitude. The basic allotment for each full-time equivalent (FTE) student in an instructional arrangement is multiplied by the appropriate weight. Each FTE is equal to thirty contact hours by students with special education personnel. The weights as they appear in House Bill 72 are as follows:

Homebound	5.0
Hospital Class.	5.0
Speech Therapy.	10.0
Resource Room	2.7
Self-Contained, Mild and Moderate, Regular Campus	2.3
Self-Contained, Severe, Regular Campus	3.5
Self-Contained, Separate Campus .	2.7
Multidistrict Class	3.5
Nonpublic Day School.	3.5
Vocational Adjustment Class . . .	2.3

```
Community Class . . . . . . . .  3.5
Self-Contained, Pregnant. . . . .  2.0
```

The new system was meant to be provisional, and the newly appointed State Board of Education was directed to formulate recommendations to modify the special education program weights. As a result, implementation of the new funding mechanism was delayed until the 1985-86 school year, and funding of special education in 1984-85 followed a modified version of the old system based on personnel units. The State Board appointed nine members to an Accountable Cost Advisory Committee, to work with the Texas Education Agency in producing a Texas Program Cost Differential Study. The purpose was to define the proper instructional arrangements for special education, ascertain the costs of each arrangement, and use these data to reformulate weights for them relative to the cost of regular education. Data on costs were obtained from a survey of one hundred school districts, selected to represent the state as a whole by size, location, wealth, and type of district, in order to develop an average cost for different instructional arrangements. These were then compared to a cost of $2,100 as the cost per student in regular education. This figure is almost $800 greater than the $1,350 basic allotment (for 1985-86) level found in House Bill 72 and was intended to represent the true cost per student in regular education rather than the lower cost supported by House Bill 72.

In the final report of the Accountable Cost Advisory Committee, the number of instructional arrangements was reduced to ten; some new arrangements were included, and the weights were generally higher than the weights found in House Bill 72.[10]

```
Regular Class Support . . . . . .  3.0
Resource Room . . . . . . . . . .  3.0
Speech Therapy. . . . . . . . . .  5.1
Partially Self-Contained. . . . .  5.1
Self-Contained, Mild/Moderate . .  5.1
Staff Intensive Self-Contained,
      Severe . . . . . . . . . .  6.9
Vocational Adjustment . . . . . .  2.4
Vocational Education
      for Handicapped. . . . . .  3.0
Hospital/Community Class. . . . .  5.1
Homebound/Homebased/Hospital
      Bedside. . . . . . . . . .  2.7
```

Vocational education for the handicapped, as shown above, was moved from the vocational education program to special education. The study also recommended that school districts be allowed to use up to 25 percent of their special education funds on "general administrative costs."

However, the methodology used in the study has been criticized by some because the sample of one hundred school districts used constitutes less than

10 percent of all districts in the state, while over one-third of all students live in them.[11]   This indicates that the largest districts were very much overrepresented. There is also concern that the data, which had to be collected in a very short time, are based on inconsistent interpretations among school district administrators who reported them, especially in the case of contact hours.

Although the State Board of Education recommended that the revised weights of the Accountable Cost Advisory Committee be adopted, the legislature did not pass these changes in the 1985 session. Therefore, the original House Bill 72 weights will remain in effect at least through 1986-87.

CONCERNS OF SCHOOL DISTRICTS

In our interviews with educators in school districts around the state, we found many differing views about the new special education funding system. In many cases, the response of administrators and teachers to the new funding mechanisms has not been enthusiastic. This coincides with much of the testimony that has been given at State Board hearings. One major concern is that the new system will result in lower funding for districts. There is also concern that the instructional arrangement weights, which direct more funds to districts that use certain instructional arrangements over others, will affect the administration of special education programs at the local level. Finally, there have been complaints about the time and effort involved in maintaining extensive records of contact hours, especially in poorer districts.

In fact, state appropriations for special education have not decreased. Appropriations for special education were $414.4 million for 1983-84 and $435.5 million for 1984-85,[12] with the latter figure almost unchanged by House Bill 72; for 1985-86, the legislature appropriated $494.8 million, with a slight increase to $505.9 million for 1986-87. Although these figures represent increases in total funding, there has been a slowdown in growth. (For example, between 1980-81 and 1981-82, state expenditures on special education increased 25 percent, from $244.1 million to $305.4 million.) Despite increases, however, state appropriations will not fully fund the amounts derived from the program weights. The Cost Differential Study noted, therefore, that some prorationing of funds for special education would be necessary.[13]   This will have the effect of reducing the weights used by a fixed percentage, undermining the intent of House Bill 72 that true cost differences between special education and regular education be reflected in state aid.

Another issue that has been of great concern is how the funding weights will affect the administration of special education programs at the district level. Because the weights try to account for the increased costs of certain instructional arrangements, some special educators fear that students will be placed in the instructional arrangement that maximizes the funds that the district will receive, rather than the arrangement which is best for the student. The House Bill 72 weights are much higher for segregated classrooms than for placement in a regular classroom, providing an incentive for districts to take handicapped children out of regular classrooms (with a weight of 1.0) and place them in self-contained classrooms (with a weight of 2.3 or 3.5). In 1985-86, such a shift would generate a minimum of $1,755 per child in additional state aid. (The incentives not to mainstream still exist in the revised weights, but at least these provide a weight of 3.0 for a handicapped child in a regular classroom, so that the incentives not to mainstream would be somewhat lower.) If these weights actually do influence placement decisions, then House Bill 72 will be in conflict with PL 94-142, the federal statute that specifically requires mainstreaming wherever possible.[14] By federal law, administrators should not make placement decisions on any grounds but the welfare of students. Many in the special education community are concerned that the mechanisms designed to prevent misplacement may be inadequate.

Finally, the amount of paperwork required by House Bill 72 has aroused some criticism. Teachers must now record the amount of time that they spend with each student in a particular instructional arrangement, as defined by the State Board. Contact hour reports from teachers are tallied by principals according to instructional arrangement. These reports are, in turn, sent to the district office, where a cumulative report is made out, and the final number of FTEs for the school district is calculated. The amount of information that House Bill 72 requires to be gathered is much greater than what was previously required. Most districts will probably not be able to hire staff to handle this work load, and the main complaint is that there will be a loss of instructional time for teachers and administrators.

CONCLUSIONS

The amount appropriated for special education by the legislature is almost sure to be less than the amount authorized in House Bill 72, especially with the revised weights recommended by the Accountable Cost Advisory Committee. Therefore, prorationing will almost certainly be necessary. The most obvious problem is that, starting from legislation which intends to provide state aid for instructional arrangements according to their real costs, prorationing dilutes the effects of cost differences. A second problem is that, although the total amount of state aid received by a district is adjusted so the poor districts receive more than wealthy districts, the allocations specifically for handicapped pupils are not adjusted for wealth.[15] Therefore, any shortfall in state funds relative to actual costs caused by prorationing will cause greater hardships in poor districts. As a result, the Equity Center has advocated that any proration be based on district wealth, rather than being an equal percentage for all districts.[16]

The issue of extensive paperwork is one that pertains to House Bill 72 in general, not just to special education. There is indeed more paperwork required of special education teachers and administrators; the question is whether, in the long run, these requirements are warranted. The forms used to keep record of contact hours are not overly complex, although it is understandable that confusion about the proper definitions of changing instructional arrangements leads to more time spent in keeping these records. As procedures become more established and special education personnel become more accustomed to them, paperwork may become less cumbersome. Nonetheless, the effect on instruction time created by record-keeping requirements should be monitored and assessed.

Finally, the possibility of discouraging mainstreaming by funding self-contained instructional arrangements at higher levels points to the potential for conflict between the goals of funding equity and of placing special education students in the least restrictive instructional arrangement possible. Whether the possibility of placing handicapped students for fiscal reasons rather than educational reasons in fact materializes depends on whether school district administrators have enough discretion to make placements in this way. Some administrators reject the notion that placement decisions could be influenced by any but legitimate educational considerations, because of federal and state regulations. The question is whether enforcement procedures currently in practice are adequate. At the moment, however, it does not seem likely that much enforcement can be expected from the federal government, and the state does not have mainstreaming requirements.

It may be that, with over a thousand school districts in Texas, enforcement is an almost impossible goal. If this is the case, funding mechanisms should be designed to <u>encourage</u> mainstreaming. One way to accomplish this would be to fund special education using different weights for different handicapping conditions rather than different instructional arrangements. This would, of course, not fund districts as accurately on the basis of cost, because of variations in instructional costs among students with the same condition. However, school districts would be encouraged to place special education students in the least expensive instructional arrangements, which would usually be the least restrictive.

Notes

[1]Education Finance Center, Education Commission of the States, Special Education Finance: The Interaction between State and Federal Support Systems, Report no. F793 (Denver, Colo.: September 1979), 1-2.

[2]Ibid.

[3]Ibid., 4.

[4]John A. Butler and Suzanne Stenmark, Evaluating the Effects of PL 94-142, the Education for All Handicapped Children Act: Working Paper (San Francisco: Institute for Health Policy Studies, School of Medicine, University of California, San Francisco, April 1982), 1.

[5]Education Finance Center, Special Education Finance, 4.

[6]Jane B. Schulz and Ann P. Turnbull, Mainstreaming Handicapped Students: A Guide for Classroom Teachers, 2nd ed. (New York: Allyn and Bacon, 1984), 56.

[7]Education Finance Center, Special Education Finance, 5.

[8]"After 17 Months, Bell Unveils Revised PL 94-142 Regulations," Phi Delta Kappan 64, (October 1982): 346.

[9]Joint Interim Committee on Special Education, Education for the Handicapped Children of Texas, 66th Texas Legislature, Austin, Texas, January 8, 1979, 9-12, 73-85.

[10]Texas Education Agency, 1984-85 Texas Program Cost Differential Study and Recommendations of the Advisory Committee for Accountable Costs to the State Board of Education, (Austin, Texas, March 1980), introduction.

[11]Ibid., 2-1.

[12]Interview with Tom Patton, State Funding, Texas Education Agency, Austin, Texas, June 28, 1985.

[13]Texas Education Agency, 1984-85 Texas Program Cost Differential Study, 5-9.

[14]The incentives to put handicapped students in special placements are not as great in the revised weights as in the original H. B. 72 weights. The revisions provide a 3.0 weight for a regular class support, where the original weights have no special provision for mainstreamed pupils.

[15]The allocations are adjusted by the PDI, however; on the average, wealthy districts tend to have higher PDIs and therefore higher allocations per handicapped pupil. As long as the PDI reflects true price differentials, these higher allocations are nominal rather than real differences.

[16]Equity Center, "Presentation to the State Board of Education," March 22, 1985.

CHAPTER SEVEN
THE EFFECTS OF HOUSE BILL 72 ON VOCATIONAL EDUCATION

The vocational education (VE) provisions of House Bill 72 changed the administration and funding of these programs in Texas. The reforms have generated considerable controversy, in part because of the strength of the VE coalition in the state and also because of disagreement about the role that VE should play in Texas's education system. The debate over vocational education is national in scope, but the SCOPE committee and House Bill 72 have heightened the controversy in Texas.

As it did for other special programs, House Bill 72 replaced earlier funding mechanisms with a provision for weighting vocational education students more than other students in calculating state aid. This approach has not only revised patterns of funding, but also changed the incentives for districts in providing different kinds of VE programs. The bill has also brought about administrative changes by requiring coordination between secondary and postsecondary programs, periodic evaluation and review, and a demonstration that the local job market can support employment in an occupation before a new course can be adopted. These policies have introduced new mechanisms of accountability to VE programs and have explicitly raised the question of goals and the effectiveness of VE programs in meeting these goals. While controversy over the appropriateness of vocational education is likely to continue, the changes in House Bill 72 provide some mechanisms for determining which VE programs are worth supporting with state revenues.

THE STRUCTURE OF VOCATIONAL EDUCATION IN TEXAS

The existing VE system in Texas is highly fragmented. There are sixteen state agencies and thirty-six boards and commissions with some responsibility for vocational education in the state. The lack of coordination among these agencies represents a serious obstacle to an effective VE program in Texas.[1]

During the 1982-83 school year, there were 497,837 VE students in grades seven to twelve. Most of these students were in home economics (39.9 percent), agriculture (12.3 percent), or industrial/technical courses (14.3 percent)[2] About 35 percent of all students in grades seven to twelve were enrolled in VE; however, many of these students were enrolled in only one or two VE courses along with their academic courses, so that the proportion of students with vocational courses as the central component of their high school program is much smaller.

For several reasons, vocational courses are more expensive than other courses. The pupil/teacher ratio is lower in VE, sometimes for safety reasons. In a thorough investigation of nineteen districts, the Texas Research League calculated that the pupil/teacher ratio in VE was about half that in other courses, 11:1 compared to 20:1.[3] VE instructors earn more than academic instructors, since they are on twelve-month rather than ten-month contracts. Furthermore, VE instructors are given double the conference periods of academic teachers. As a result, the Texas Research League determined that the average cost per pupil of a VE course was $423, compared to a cost of $181 for academic core courses and $215 for noncore academic courses.

Although these cost figures are only suggestive, there is little question that VE is more expensive than other programs. As a result, the question of whether these costs are worthwhile has been raised frequently. Nationally, the effectiveness of vocational education has come under increasing criticism, partly because a long series of evaluations has consistently demonstrated that vocational programs do not give students any employment advantages.[4] Many of the recent reports criticizing education have called for efforts to strengthen academic education, and several have explicitly called for the elimination of vocational education.[5]

In Texas, the head of the Select Committee on Public Education, H. Ross Perot, was a vociferous critic of vocational education during SCOPE hearings in 1983, using anecdotal evidence to make the same points about the ineffectiveness of VE programs. As a result, SCOPE did not recommend funding for VE. The changes in House Bill 72 therefore represent a compromise, continuing state funding for VE but with a series of administrative changes to increase the accountability of VE programs.

CHANGES IN FINANCING VOCATIONAL EDUCATION

Perhaps the most controversial change put into effect by House Bill 72 is the new funding formula established for VE in Texas. Under prior law, state funds were allocated based on the personnel employed by the districts for VE programs. This ensured that districts could fund programs for which instructors were hired, regardless of enrollment levels, and the funding mechanism encouraged low pupil/teacher ratios. House Bill 72 distributes funds based on the number of full-time equivalent (FTE) students enrolled in VE programs. A student with at least thirty hours of contact per week with a VE instructor is counted as an FTE, while a student with at least fifteen hours a week is considered half an FTE.

Under the new legislation, every FTE student in vocational education is given a weight of 1.45 in calculating state aid. The weight of 1.45 was established to increase VE funding by 5 percent, a modest increase, given the overall increase in state aid of about 20 percent in House Bill 72. This supplement of .45 was worth $581 in 1984-85 for the lowest-cost districts; since the basic allotment for districts varies with the price differential index, the VE supplement was $708 in the highest-cost districts with a PDI of 1.291. The bill requires that this weight be applied to all VE students regardless of the type of VE course they take. This aspect of the formula has come under considerable criticism, since costs for VE vary depending on the types of programs offered by districts. Some districts fear that more expensive courses may need to be discontinued, since they will be underfunded by the 1.45 weight.

For other special programs, House Bill 72 allowed districts to use state funds to cover administrative costs. However, the legislation did not include such a provision for VE funds allocated by the new formula. Finally, the new legislation required that the State Board establish minimum enrollment levels for VE courses and specified that a district's VE funds will be decreased if these enrollment levels are not met.

Although House Bill 72 did not consider variation in costs among different vocational programs, it did require that costs be studied and recommendations for revised weights be made. In March 1985, TEA published the Cost Differential Study as required by House Bill 72.[6] The recommendations call for the establishment of four VE weights to take account of variation in program costs. Vocational classroom instruction and general occupational training would receive a weight of 1.5. Vocational cooperative programs would be given a weight of 1.4, while occupational cluster programs and vocational-technical training would be given weights of 1.7 and 1.9, respectively. The study also recommended that the basic allotment be raised to $2,100. The study projected that the cost of these weights applied to the $1,350 basic allotment for 1985-86 would be $248.1 million, while the higher base of $2,100 would increase costs by almost 68 percent, to $415.7 million. The study also indicated that small rural districts have the highest proportion of their students in VE courses.[7] Thus, it is important to develop a clear understanding of how these districts have been affected by changes in the VE funding formula.

Although the State Board of Education recommended that these new weights be adopted, the failure of any revisions to House Bill 72 to pass during the 1985 legislative session means that the single weight of 1.45 will remain in force at least through 1986-87. As we describe below, this weights mechanism creates incentives that many vocational educators fear will be detrimental to successful programs.

ADMINISTRATIVE CHANGES

One of the most important administrative changes of House Bill 72 calls for sunset review of VE programs every five years. House Bill 72 also calls for on-site review of local programs at least every five years. Both provisions imply that districts will have to evaluate their VE programs more carefully than in the past, and the sunset review implies that ineffective programs will be eliminated. The legislation does not provide any guidance about either review procedure, although the State Board of Education has the power to develop guidelines for such reviews.

Before criteria can be established for evaluating VE programs, the goals of VE must be made explicit. House Bill 72 requires that the State Board establish a master plan for VE to articulate the objectives of the state's program for the following year. This plan should play an important part in determining how VE programs are reviewed in accordance with the sunset provision of the law.

VE programs are generally intended to provide skills that will enable students to enter the job market in a related field upon graduation from high school. However, the information about local labor market conditions in vocational programs is often quite weak;[8] stories are legion of VE programs "training for unemployment" because there are not jobs in the occupations for which students are trained. House Bill 72 requires that new course offerings in VE be supported by local job market surveys. These surveys are to be used to indicate which VE skills will be needed to fill expected vacancies in the local job market.

House Bill 72 also calls for improved articulation between secondary schools and postsecondary vocational institutions, including the community colleges and the four Texas state technical institutes. Such coordination is meant to ensure that overlap in course offerings is minimized among schools teaching similar VE courses in a given district. This provision will be relevant only for those districts that are reasonably close to postsecondary institutions; but since both community colleges and high school students are concentrated in urban areas, only districts in rural areas should be unable to coordinate with postsecondary institutions. Although some districts have already established coordinating mechanisms, there are currently no standard procedures for detecting course overlap or dividing responsibility for VE between secondary and postsecondary institutions.

To facilitate greater flexibility in course offerings, House Bill 72 allows for ten-, eleven-, or twelve-month contracts for VE instructors. This will enable districts to hire temporary instructors so that VE courses can be more sensitive to the changes in local labor markets. Districts have also been given the flexibility to use VE instructors to teach non-VE courses for which they are qualified, and VE facilities may be utilized for non-VE activities when needed. Finally, House Bill 72 requires that every VE program in the state offer competency-based instruction and that student competency profiles be established for each student.

Clearly, most of the administrative changes in House Bill 72 are intended to improve the effectiveness of vocational programs, by eliminating ineffective programs by providing the information to allow educators to know whether programs are working, by preventing unnecessary programs from being created, and by allowing greater flexibility and coordination. This emphasis on effectiveness is especially welcome because of the implications of the evaluations of VE programs: the finding that VE has no economic effects on the average does not imply that all VE programs are ineffective, but probably that effective programs coexist with worthless ones.[9] The changes in House Bill 72 should enable educators to distinguish the worthwhile programs from those that "train for unemployment" and thereby to strengthen vocational education as a whole.

THE RESPONSE OF DISTRICTS TO THE VOCATIONAL EDUCATIONAL
PROVISIONS OF HOUSE BILL 72

In our interviews in school districts, vocational educators frequently criticized the single weight of 1.45 for VE students, because it does not take variation in costs of VE programs into account. For example, 1982 data indicate that per pupil expenditures ranged from a low of $83.68 for exploratory programs to a high of $618.60 for technical course offerings.[10] Because the costs of capital-intensive VE courses such as shop and mechanics are higher than the costs of classroom-based courses such as home economics, educators fear that more expensive courses will be squeezed out. Because the legislature did not adopt multiple weights recommended by the Accountable Cost Advisory Committee and the State Board of Education, the rigidity of the single weight will continue in effect for at least two more years. One issue is to continue monitoring what kinds of vocational programs are reduced or eliminated because of this weighting mechanism.

Based on interviews, it is clear that some (but not all) districts lost money under the new weighting process, despite statewide increases in VE funding. Many vocational educators reported that class size in VE programs would increase, both because of the decrease in funding experienced by some districts and because funding on the basis of pupils (rather than personnel units or teachers) encourages higher pupil/teacher ratios. On the one hand, this incentive should operate to reduce the high per pupil costs of VE. On the other hand, some VE instructors were concerned that class size should be limited in some courses for safety reasons and suggested that minimum enrollment requirements should also be sensitive to safety issues.

Vocational educators in several districts indicated that they do make an effort to develop course offerings based on local employment needs. However, those districts that do so have no uniformity in how they conduct labor market surveys. Districts also vary with respect to the involvement of the private sector in determining local market needs. Some efforts survey local businesses, while others include the participation of local representatives of the federal Job Training Partnership Act (JTPA) program. While this variation may also make uniform implementation difficult on a statewide basis, it also confirms the need for some state standards and technical assistance in methods of determining demand for VE programs.

A final problem reported by some (although not all) vocational educators arises from the curriculum changes of House Bill 246. Because the new curriculum requirements emphasize academic coursework, some VE instructors feared that students would have less time for vocational programs. To some, the combination of funding pressures in House Bill 72, new administrative requirements, and a bias against vocational education in House Bill 246 constitutes a consistent attack, and they feel that the state's encouragement of vocational programs, shown in its commitment to area vocational schools during the 1970s, is now dwindling.

Overall, sentiments among vocational educators varied about the effect of

SCOPE and House Bill 72 on VE in Texas. Most felt that the criticisms of H. Ross Perot and others were based on a few bad cases or on a lack of knowledge about VE in the state. On the other hand, others felt that the criticism helped to focus attention on VE. This increased attention not only brought some of the problems facing VE to light, but also mobilized support for the program and led to changes that over the long run may strengthen vocational education.

CONCLUSIONS AND RECOMMENDATIONS

The present funding system using a weight of 1.45 is likely to cause some serious problems unless it is changed to better reflect cost differentials by program type and location. The funding issue is especially important when one considers that technical VE programs are the most expensive to establish, and in many cases these will be the most important offerings for meeting local job market needs--more important, given the direction of the Texas economy, than homemaking or agriculture. Unless weights are appropriately set, it may prove difficult to meet the most pressing job needs in some parts of the state. Over the next several years, it is important to monitor changes in VE offerings, to see exactly how the revised VE funding mechanisms affect the types of programs and how they affect districts of different size and wealth.

The data also indicate that some courses should be cut back or eliminated. This is especially true of agricultural VE, since this sector is likely to decline in the near future but continues to make up a substantial proportion of total VE students in the state;[11] home economics is another area of VE with high enrollments (nearly 40 percent of all vocational students) but with an avocational purpose at best. Reducing certain kinds of courses, like other applications of the new sunset provisions in House Bill 72, can be facilitated through the use of rigorous job market evaluation at the local level.

The success of the provisions set forth in House Bill 72 for VE will depend on proper implementation and enforcement. This is especially true for assessments of local labor market needs. Uniform criteria should be established to guide assessment of local program needs, to facilitate the collection of statewide information, and to ensure that assessments and evaluations are based on valid criteria throughout the state. A sincere commitment to a degree of uniformity will require that the state provide technical assistance to small districts without the resources to develop appropriate evaluation instruments.

The finance provisions of House Bill 72 for VE in Texas are designed to fund relatively specific program areas based on local labor market needs. However, a long series of reports has criticized VE for narrow skill training and argued that more emphasis should be placed on general skills so that graduates are more adaptable to changing labor market conditions.[12] In fact, federal legislation enacted in 1984, reauthorizing the Vocational Education Act, stressed "the capability of vocational education programs to meet the needs for several occupational skills and improvement of academic foundations in order to address the changing content of work"; the conference report accompanying the final bill contains more precise recommendations for making vocational education more general.

In assessing the capability of programs for special needs groups and the general vocational student population in meeting general occupational skills and improvement of academic foundations, states shall assess whether the programs use problem solving and basic skills (including mathematics, reading, writing, science, and social studies) in the vocational setting. It is the intent to give a student experience in and understanding of all aspects of the industry in which the student is preparing to enter.[13]

This suggests that the VE curriculum at the high school level should be relatively general, with an increase in specificity in later years--for example, in the community colleges. (In fact, the recommendations of a recent major study of Texas VE are consistent with this philosophy.)[14] The various mechanisms of accountability established by House Bill 72 should help more districts in this direction.

In general, the provisions of House Bill 72 related to vocational education are a compromise between critics (like H. Ross Perot) who would like to see state aid for VE abolished and advocates who tend to feel that VE should be expanded with few controls. If it is properly implemented, the compromise should be a constructive approach to the dilemma of whether vocational programs are worthwhile, by providing districts and the state with the mechanisms to improve evaluations, accountability, and labor market information. If these are taken seriously, the result would be a substantial improvement in a program that has all too often been under fire.

Notes

[1]Research Triangle Institute, Final Technical Report: A Study to Make Recommendations Regarding a Comprehensive State Occupational Education Program (Research Triangle Park, N. C., October 31, 1982), 43.

[2]Texas Education Association, "Vocational Education in Texas," undated.

[3]Texas Research League, Resource Allocation in Texas School Districts: A Functional Cost Analysis, Preliminary Report (Austin, Texas: Texas Research League, March 9, 1984) iv.

[4]For evaluations of vocational education, see Robert Meyer and David Wise, "High School Preparation and Early Labor Force Experience," The Youth Labor Market Problem: Its Nature, Causes, and Consequences, ed. Richard Freeman and David Wise (Chicago: University of Chicago Press, 1982), 277-347; Russ Rumberger and Thomas Daymont, "The Economic Value of Academic and Vocational Training Acquired in High School," Youth and the Labor Market: Analyses of the National Longitudinal Survey ed. Michael E. Borus (Kalamazoo, Mich.: W. E. Upjohn Institute for Employment Research, 1984), 157-92; John Grasso and John Shear, Vocational Education and Training: Impact on Youth (Berkeley: Carnegie Council on Policy Studies in Higher Education, 1979); and Beatrice Reubens, "Vocational Education for All in High School?" in Janice O'Toole, Work and the Quality of Life (Cambridge: MIT Press, 1974).

[5]See especially Ernest Boyer, High School: A Report on Secondary Education in America (New York: Harper and Row, 1983). In response to these criticisms, vocational educators have defended their programs in the National Commission on Secondary Vocational Education, The Unfinished Agenda: The Role of Vocational Education in the High School (Columbus, Ohio: National Center for Research in Vocational Education, 1985).

[6]Texas Education Agency, 1984-85 Texas Program Cost Differential Study and Recommendations of the Advisory Committee for Accountable Costs to the State Board of Education (Austin, Texas, March 8, 1985).

[7]Ibid., 1-11.

[8]Robert Taylor, Howard Rosen, and Frank Pratzner, eds., The Responsiveness of Training Institutions to Changing Labor Market Demand (Columbus, Ohio: National Center for Research in Vocational Education, 1982).

[9]For this interpretation, see W. Norton Grubb, "The Phoenix of Vocational Education: Implications Evaluation," in The Planning Papers for the Vocational Education Study, Vocational Education Study, Publication no. 1 (Washington, D.C.: National Institute of Education, 1979).

[10]Advisory Council for Technical-Vocational Education in Texas, <u>Moving Ahead in Vocational Education: 14th Annual Report to the State Board for Technical-Vocational Education in Texas</u> (Austin, Texas, December 1983), 2.

[11]Research Triangle Institute, <u>Final Technical Report</u>, 47.

[12]Grubb, "The Phoenix of Vocational Education."

[13]House Report no. 98-1129, 98th Cong., 2d sess., vol. 136, no. 128, Oct. 2, 1984, <u>Congressional Record</u>, H 10783.

[14]"Texas Attempts to Align Vocational Education with Employer Needs", <u>Hypotenuse</u>, Research Triangle Institute (January/February, 1983).

CHAPTER EIGHT
IMPLEMENTING NEW PROGRAMS:
THE PREKINDERGARTEN AND SUMMER PRESCHOOL PROGRAMS

Many of the new requirements in House Bill 72 attempt to improve existing programs and facilities. The bill also introduced new programs intended to meet the future needs of students, including technology education, prekindergarten, and summer preschool. Implementing new programs presents more problems than reforming existing programs; although there are no established practices to be overcome, there may be little enthusiasm and no established constituency supporting an innovation. Indeed, the need for state (or federal) initiative often arises because local districts do not provide for a potentially valuable program, implying that new programs are likely to meet either indifference or hostility.

The purpose of the technology education program encouraged in House Bill 72 is to supply students with skills in mathematics, science, computer science, and other related subjects to prepare them for the "New Age." These programs were neither funded nor required by the legislature, and specific details about the program were left to the discretion of the districts. Districts in Texas are preoccupied with meeting the requirements of House Bill 72; while they show real interest in technology education, few of the districts we interviewed have taken any steps to develop such a program. Without funding, state requirements, or technical assistance, it is unclear what the "encouragement" of House Bill 72 means, and it seems likely that only the wealthier districts and those located in urban areas with substantial growth in high-technology employment will be likely to respond.

The legislature followed a different approach by requiring prekindergarten programs and summer preschool programs of certain districts. Both programs intend to prepare children for their primary years of public school education; both are efforts to extend the years of schooling to younger children, much as the kindergarten extended public education from six- to five-year-olds. The preschool programs of House Bill 72 are of particular note, because they reflect a growing interest around the country in early childhood education as an effective method of compensatory education. In this chapter we examine the early responses of districts to these novel programs and suggest various ways of improving them.

THE PREKINDERGARTEN PROGRAM

Many children begin kindergarten or the first grade "educationally disadvantaged." A limited vocabulary, an inability to speak English proficiently, or the absence of early childhood educational and developmental stimuli may have contributed to their disadvantaged state. As a result, they are often unable to keep pace with their peers, and efforts to begin their schooling earlier to compensate have a long history (including kindergarten itself).[1]

The prekindergarten program is one way to compensate disadvantaged children through a half-day, full-year, voluntary program for four-year-olds who are limited English proficient or come from low-income families as defined by eligibility for the school lunch program.[2] Districts having fifteen or more such children <u>must</u> offer the program beginning in 1985-86, while other districts <u>may</u> offer it if they choose. Once the educationally disadvantaged have been served, districts may allow other four-year-olds to participate as well.[3] However, districts that must construct new facilities may apply to TEA for a waiver of the prekindergarten requirement.

The program expenses will be shared by the state and the local district, according to a formula which provides a greater fraction of state support for poor districts. For 1985-86, the legislature has appropriated $45 million, a sum that puts Texas in second place (California is first) among states in state funding for early childhood education.[4] However, if large numbers of children attend and the appropriation is insufficient, districts will receive only a fraction of the aid they would otherwise receive. As a result, there is substantial uncertainty about how much aid the state will provide for prekindergarten.

Although Texas has never before <u>required</u> its districts to provide preschool programs, it does have a history of promoting preschool services for other special populations. One such program was the Preschool Deaf Program, introduced by the legislature in 1959.[5] The purpose was to prepare deaf children for Texas schools or the Texas School for the Deaf, through development of communication skills. Another preschool program, funded by federal Title I funds, was the Preschool Program for Migrant Children, which was offered during the regular school year. When this program was introduced in 1967-68, kindergarten programs were not required by the state, and five-year-olds were considered preschool children. The program was combined with the state kindergarten program at the end of the 1970-71 school year.[6]

In addition, a number of early childhood bilingual programs have been developed by districts using funds available under Title VII of the Elementary and Secondary Education Act. Children aged three through five who are limited English proficient and are from low-income families are eligible.[7] Head Start, a federally funded preschool program for low-income children, is provided through some school districts. Finally, in 1969, the legislature authorized a preschool program for "exceptional" children.[8] Handicapped children aged three through five were eligible for the program. As the federal funds for many of these services were decreased or eliminated, many preschool programs were discontinued by the districts, which could not afford to fund them locally. As a result, most districts did not offer any preschool at the time House Bill 72 was adopted. However, some districts did have model preschool programs, and the reasons for their existence and their structure are instructive; an appendix to this chapter describes these model programs.

The Select Committee on Public Education should be credited with the inception of the prekindergarten program. The need for early childhood education was confirmed by teachers, principals, and administrators across the state who were interviewed by SCOPE members.[9] Two members of SCOPE were especially strong advocates of preschool programs--Dr. Emette J. Conrad, a Dallas surgeon, and Dr. Elizabeth MacNaughton, a Houston psychiatrist. Partly because of their support, SCOPE made these recommendations:

1. Early childhood care and education programs in Texas should be improved in "quality and availability."

2. The state should participate in the regulation of the curriculum, as well as the physical structure of day care centers in Texas.

3. Public schools should participate in the provision of parenthood programs.

The legislature responded to the first of these recommendations by enacting the prekindergarten program. Since public schools in Texas were only recently required to provide kindergarten programs, the adoption of preschool education programs by the legislature was somewhat surprising. However, the Texas legislature reflects a growing potential interest in early childhood programs as effective forms of compensatory education. Extensive publicity about the positive effects of Head Start and of the Perry Preschool program, a small experimental preschool that has boasted benefit-cost ratios of seven to one,[10] have increased public awareness of early childhood education.

REACTIONS OF SCHOOL DISTRICTS

Of the districts we surveyed, more than half plan to implement the prekindergarten program in the fall of 1985, as required. But these districts typically have had some experience with preschool education. Many had previously offered a program, like the preschool program for migrant children, or were affiliated with a program like Head Start. A few of the districts currently offer a preschool program for the same children targeted by the legislation. In addition to having preschool experience, these districts usually have administrative and staff personnel committed to the concept of early childhood education. Finally, the districts quickest to implement the prekindergarten requirement have classroom space available or are able to obtain the necessary space.

However, compliance will be difficult for most districts regardless of size, wealth, or location. The primary deterrent to compliance for many districts is a shortage of classrooms. Some districts, like Brownsville ISD, have experienced tremendous growth and faced classroom shortages even prior to H.B. 72.[11] Others require more space because of new maximum class size in kindergarten through grade two, so that the prekindergarten program must compete for space with other requirements of House Bill 72. In some cases, the number of additional classrooms needed for the prekindergarten program is substantial. El Paso is now building fifty-seven new classrooms to accommodate a population of approximately 1,700 four-year-olds who will qualify for the program.[12] Austin plans to expand its existing programs by fifty classrooms as soon as it can build the space.[13]

Some districts (like Weslaco ISD) have large numbers of vacant classrooms. For these districts, a teacher shortage will be the most serious problem.[14] Hiring qualified teachers will be especially difficult for the larger districts, which need a large proportion of the teachers available. Approximately 1,170 new teachers graduate each year in Texas with early childhood education certificates. To satisfy the program requirements, Houston ISD alone will need one-half of these graduates.[15]

Finally, funding has been of concern to all districts. The costs of the programs are not by any means trivial; for example, Houston ISD estimates that the program will cost the district approximately $5.2 million, not including capital expenses for furniture and facilities.[16] During the 1984-85 school year, the legislature did not appropriate any money for the prekindergarten program, and it was unclear whether the 1985 legislature would abolish it under fiscal pressures, provide the full $50 million allowed in House Bill 72, or take an intermediate course. Many districts adopted a wait-and-see attitude during the 1984-85 school year, regardless of size or wealth. As a result, there was little planning for the prekindergarten program before the summer of 1985.

In addition to these tangible obstacles, we found that attitudes toward the concept of early childhood education are also potential impediments. Most districts will implement the new program because they must, not because they are enthusiastic about preschool education. The concept of early childhood education was understood and appreciated by most district superintendents, and many indicated some knowledge of research in the field. However, their overriding concern was how to finance the program in addition to other requirements of House Bill 72. Attitudes ranged from an emphatic "we'll only offer it if we have to!" to what one administrator called "neutral enthusiasm." Several administrators also expressed concern that the state may be in the process of redefining the role of the public schools to include childraising, a responsibility some thought more appropriate to parents. "Are we going to begin taking them from the cradle?" was a question posed by a superintendent of a small district.

Others claimed that the state-mandated programs were decreasing local control. These administrators contend that the prekindergarten program is not really needed in their districts, because existing programs adequately meet the needs of the local community. And some district administrators admitted doubts about the effectiveness of early childhood programs. A few administrators expressed real excitement about expanding education to four-year-olds, but they were largely in districts which already had a similar program. Small, rural districts expressed the greatest hesitancy about the program, because funding is uncertain and the number of eligible children will probably be small.

DISTRICT COMPLIANCE WITH THE PREKINDERGARTEN REQUIREMENT

Many of the districts which plan to offer the program in the fall of 1985 have been actively surveying the community to identify eligible children. Some have informed the local community of the new program through letters or brochures, while others have run advertisements in the local newspapers. But a number of districts had not informed the local community as of the spring of 1985, pending further legislative decisions. They were apprehensive about promoting a program which might not come to fruition.

Besides doing surveys, many districts have also been recruiting new teachers. Higher salaries, better working conditions, and bonuses are some of the devices districts have used to combat teacher shortages and lure available faculty to their schools. For example, Houston ISD has considered offering a $1,500 bonus to colleges and universities for each student agreeing to teach in HISD.[17]

Finally, districts which plan to offer prekindergarten in fall 1985 have been selecting classroom sites. Some must obtain portable classrooms until new ones are constructed, while others plan to use community churches and other facilities to accommodate the children while classrooms are under construction. Many districts without unused classroom space have passed new bond issues or plan to do so. Most are planning to build new classrooms, and some (like La Vernia ISD), new schools.[18]

It appears that most school districts will not deviate from the minimum requirements suggested by the legislature. Most programs will run half-day, full-year programs, with a pupil/teacher ratio of 22:1. (This ratio, the same maximum required for kindergarten through second grade, was adopted for the prekindergarten by the Texas Education Agency.) Aides will probably not be used in most districts. In most cases the program will be located within walking distance of eligible children; although transportation is not required by House Bill 72, many districts will provide it for those children living outside a two-mile radius from the school.

Those districts unable to comply with the program requirements for the fall of 1985 because of a classroom shortage qualify for the "construction waiver." However, the exemption is not a permanent provision. State Board rulings have clarified that districts will have a maximum of three years to build facilities to fulfill the program requirements.[19] In addition, districts must develop plans demonstrating how the prekindergarten program will be phased in over the three-year period. Finally, exemptions will only be granted to those districts which demonstrate they have thoroughly searched for other possible facilities. Since many districts have no unused classrooms available or must use additional classrooms to meet the maximum class size, it may be at least three years before the prekindergarten program is finally implemented.

THE QUALITY OF THE PREKINDERGARTEN PROGRAM

While the legislature has attempted to address the needs of preschool children through the prekindergarten program, the program enacted may not be effective in assisting the very children it was designed to serve. For a combination of reasons--including fiscal constraints, the time pressures associated with implementing House Bill 72, the basic structure of the prekindergarten program, and simple unfamiliarity with early childhood education within the schools and TEA--the prekindergarten program could develop in ways detrimental to its intentions.

It is first necessary to understand what makes an early childhood education program successful. A report prepared by the U.S. Department of Health, Education and Welfare identifies some of the characteristics of successful preschool programs, including:

1. Careful planning and a clear statement of academic objectives.

2. Small groups and a high degree of individualization of instruction.

3. Instruction and materials relevant and closely related to objectives.

4. High intensity of treatment.

5. Teacher training in the methods of the program.[20]

One of the most successful preschool programs, the Perry Preschool Projects, included 123 children from 1962 through 1967, in the Perry Elementary School in Ypsilanti, Michigan. The children included were black, had IQs between 70 and 85, and were from families with low socioeconomic status.[21] Careful evaluation has demonstrated that children in the program needed less remedial education and were held back less often than similar children not included; scholastic achievement was improved, high school graduation rates were higher, delinquency rates lower, and rates of employment following graduation higher.[22] But while many people have been made aware of these findings and are familiar with the much-publicized benefit-cost ratio of seven to one, few are aware of the quality of the program. It was carefully developed by child psychologists and child developmental specialists; the staff was well trained and enthusiastic, the teachers' salaries were competitive with the local public schools, and the pupil/teacher ratio was very low, approximately 5:1 or 6:1.[23] Four teachers typically supervised twenty to twenty-five children. In 1985 dollars, the program cost about $5,000 per pupil.[24]

Head Start is another example of a preschool program with positive outcomes that have become widely known. Head Start was developed over a period of years and attracted the attention of the entire child development community; in many ways it was a "laboratory" for early childhood education in this century. A federally funded program, Head Start was introduced during the 1960s as part of President Johnson's War on Poverty.[25] Unlike many early childhood plans, Head Start is a comprehensive program which combines a number of components, including health services, social services, early childhood education, parent involvement, a volunteer effort, community participation, career ladders, and in-service training.[26] The pupil/teacher ratio for the Head Start program is also low, about 5:1. One teacher and two aides typically supervise fifteen children. The average cost per child in 1984 was about $2,700, a figure that included some part-time programs; thus, the cost of a full-day program is close to $4,000. Other exemplary programs include the California Children's Centers, which are full-day programs for low-income children, operated through public schools; the pupil teacher ratio is 8:1, and the cost per child in 1984-85 averaged $4,400.

Still other evidence about the quality of early childhood education comes from the National Day Care Study.[27] This study examined the determinants of quality in day care centers, and concluded that pupil/teacher ratios between 5:1 and 10:1 made little difference to quality, recommending that ratios be between 8:1 and 10:1. Above 10:1, however, quality began to deteriorate, and above 20:1 there was evidence that a center could be harmful to young children.

Thus, the model early childhood programs--the basis for the publicity about the benefits of educating young children--all have ratios around 6:1 and costs between $4,000 and $5,000 for a full day. In contrast, SCOPE recommended pupil/teacher ratios of 15:1, far in excess of levels recommended by child development research, and these were further diluted to 22:1. Administrators of existing prekindergarten programs in Austin and Fort Worth agree that this ratio is too high, because of the individual attention those four-year-olds require; Austin plans to maintain a 16:1 ratio, and Fort Worth--which has provided a prekindergarten program for more than fourteen years--uses a pupil/teacher ratio of 11:1.[28]

Another issue related to quality involves training of teachers for preschool programs. The teachers in the Perry Preschool, Head Start, and the California Children's Centers have all had extensive training in child development and early childhood education, and the National Day Care Study confirmed that specific training in early childhood education--rather than increased levels of education in general--enhanced quality. However, Texas has recently diluted its training requirements for teachers of young children. Prior to 1983, a teacher of young children (TYC) certificate was necessary to teach kindergarten and was considered a model certificate by early childhood experts. In 1983, the Commission on Standards of the Teacher Profession of TEA attempted to abolish the TYC certificate, not for educational reasons but to provide administrators greater flexibility in assigning teachers. After protests by the early childhood community, a compromise certificate was developed, known as option 4 of the regular elementary education certificate. This certificate, valid for prekindergarten through grade six, does require some training in early childhood, but, since it must cover topics ranging up to grade six, it dilutes the content of the old TYC certificate.[29]

Another problem involves the length of the program day. SCOPE committee members suggested a seven-hour school day for the prekindergarten program, including lunch and rest periods. Instead, the legislature mandated a half-day program with a minimum requirement of three hours. Aside from providing more time in the program, the full-day program would have allowed the districts to schedule the transportation of the four-year-olds at the same time as the other students, while the half-day prekindergarten program may cause scheduling problems for many districts (as the half-day kindergarten program currently does). A more serious consequence is that parents unable or unwilling to provide transportation for their children may exclude them from prekindergarten.

The three-hour program also precludes the attendance of eligible children who have working parents, unless their parents can arrange coordinated child care. In fact, some districts have experienced high absenteeism in their kindergarten programs because so many children have working parents.[30] Austin administrators plan to continue a full-day prekindergarten because they fear too many children will be unable to attend a three-hour program.[31] In Texas, 49 percent of all mothers with children under six work, and for women without a husband present--the group that includes many eligible for prekindergarten--68 percent of mothers with young children work.[32] For these children, a three-hour program may not be a real opportunity.

A final problem is the lack of technical assistance. Almost all districts in Texas are unfamiliar with early childhood education; TEA has no experience or expertise in this area and can only suggest their districts examine a model program--the one in Austin--when they ask for assistance. The exemplary programs, like Head Start and Perry Preschool, have drawn heavily on the expertise of child development experts and the California Children's Centers similarly have substantial assistance available from the State Department of Education. Especially for a new program, the lack of technical assistance could be crucial.

The good intentions of SCOPE in recommending the prekindergarten program and of the legislature in passing House Bill 72 are unmistakable. However, the programs that begin in the fall of 1985 are unlikely to look much like the exemplary programs for low-income children that have motivated the interest in early childhood education. Subsequent efforts of the State Board of Education and the Texas legislature should investigate the quality of this program more carefully.

THE SUMMER PRESCHOOL PROGRAM

A second preschool program for the educationally disadvantaged also emerged from House Bill 72. The summer preschool program is an eight-week, half-day, voluntary program for students of limited English proficiency who will enter kindergarten or the first grade; it is therefore open to five-and-six-year-olds. This program must be offered by those districts currently required to offer bilingual or special language programs for K-12 students. The legislation also stipulates that the pupil/teacher ratio may not exceed 18:1, and the program must be offered during the eight-week period preceding the start of the regular school year.

The summer program was not included in the recommendations of the Select Committee on Public Education. TEA administrators in the Division of Bilingual Education admitted they were surprised to see the program included in the bill.[33] However, the logic of the program is similar to that of the prekindergarten program. The roots of this program can be traced to a similar program authorized by the legislature during the late 1950s. While not a bilingual program or a required program, the objective of the Preschool Instructional Program for Non-English Speaking Children was to improve the communication skills of children unable to speak and understand the English language.[34] Children ready to enter the first grade were eligible. The philosophy of the program was that improved communication skills would reduce the dropout rate and prevent more expensive remediation later.[35] The cost of the program was shared by the state and participating districts. The program was eventually discontinued during the mid-1970s because it was superseded by bilingual programs supported by federal funds as well as those required by the state legislation and by the extension of the kindergarten program to all children.[36]

All districts required to provide the summer preschool program in the summer of 1985 plan to comply with the new legislation. While most of these districts have never offered a bilingual summer program for four-year-olds, many have provided some type of summer language program such as ESL or Chapter 1 migrant summer school programs for children of other ages. However, many districts--those not required to provide a bilingual program or which do not have at least fifteen eligible children--will not offer the program because they are exempt. Most of the exempt districts only offer an ESL program.

Because this program is to be offered during the summer, classroom shortages will not pose a problem. Most districts have solicited their existing bilingual faculties to teach the summer program and have received positive responses. However, some districts expressed concern that teachers may be difficult to hire. One reason is that teachers who want to advance on the career ladder will need the summer months to attend classes. Some districts--especially those in the Valley, like Brownsville, where 87 percent of the children are Hispanic--may have difficulties because of the large number of teachers needed to operate the program. Urban districts with large bilingual populations, like Houston, could also have staffing problems. Approximately 555 teachers are needed for Houston's preschool summer program, while the annual number of new teachers graduating with bilingual certification is only 300.[37] To meet its staffing needs, the district mailed applications to all bilingual teachers now working in the district. Kindergarten and first grade teachers, as well as those with prior early childhood education experience, will be given first priority.

One potential impediment to implementation for most districts seems to be a lack of funding. The 1985 legislature appropriated $5.7 million for 1985-86 and $6.0 million for 1986-87 for the summer preschool programs. These funds are estimated to be sufficient to cover all the costs of the program in the 183 districts that will be required to provide one; districts will be reimbursed $1,750 for every class of eighteen children covering a half-day, eight-week program.[38] If these funds are insufficient or if districts want to expand the program beyond the minimum level required, they may use state bilingual funds, state compensatory education funds, federal bilingual, Chapter 1 migrant, or regular state and local funds to finance the program. The adequacy of the legislative appropriation is not entirely clear. Depending upon the size of the eligible preschool population, many districts may be forced to use local revenues to finance the program. Accordingly, those districts with the largest populations of bilingual students--which tend to have low property values per pupil--will bear the greatest financial burdens. For districts like El Paso, with approximately two thousand eligible children, and Houston, which has approximately ten thousand eligible children, state financial assistance is crucial.

As in the case of the prekindergarten program, uncertainty about funding led some districts to wait until the 1985 legislative session clarified the funding provisions; these districts were apprehensive about planning and advertising a program that might be postponed or eliminated. Most districts we surveyed planned to offer the program to all eligible students. But some districts will offer the program only to a specific number of students because of financial constraints. Eligible students unable to attend will be put on a waiting list.

The most positive responses to the summer preschool program came from those districts with large populations of Spanish-speaking students, where there is great need for the program. In districts like Weslaco, some students will not speak English until they enter school.[39] However, some districts were apprehensive about the effectiveness of a "crash" summer program. Much of the hesitancy was expressed by the smaller districts which have few eligible students. Some of these administrators believe the program is not really needed in their particular districts because services currently provided are adequate. Others expressed concern that young children would be in school for too long a period.

Many districts plan to follow the program structure as mandated by the state. Most districts will keep the pupil/teacher ratio at 18:1, but some do plan to use aides as well. However, some districts (like Brazosport ISD) believe the legislated ratio is too high for the program to be effective and will use a lower ratio instead.[40] As in the prekindergarten program, the appropriate pupil/teacher ratio remains a critical issue, because many educators feel that it is central to the success of the program. Unfortunately, there has been so little experience with summer bilingual preschools that there is no evidence to suggest what ratios should be.

Even though districts are not required to do so, many plan to provide transportation, because they fear that attendance will suffer otherwise. For example, the superintendent of the Taylor ISD, which already provides a four-week summer remedial program for children, commented that even with transportation many students fail to attend classes because of a lack of parental support; without transportation the problem would be worse.[41]   Those districts which will not provide transportation plan to locate the program in schools within walking distance of most eligible children.

A final concern is the timing of the program, which must be provided during the eight weeks preceding the regular school year. Districts like Weslaco, which has the second largest migrant population in the state, fear that the migrant children will not be able to participate in the program because they will be out of town.[42]

CONCLUSIONS AND RECOMMENDATIONS

The conditions influencing implementation of the prekindergarten requirements are really no different than those affecting other House Bill 72 requirements. Uncertain funding, shortages of teachers, and a lack of classrooms are the problems experienced by most districts regardless of size, wealth, or location. In particular, the prekindergarten program will compound the classroom shortage, which has been greatly intensified because of the 22:1 pupil/teacher ratio requirement for grades K-2. Those districts near or at capacity will have to build additional classrooms and perhaps even entire schools.

Most districts offering the prekindergarten and preschool summer programs will do so because they must and not necessarily because they are enthusiastic about early childhood education. While many district administrators believe the programs have merit, the major concern is how to finance the programs in addition to the other House Bill 72 requirements. Not surprisingly, the few districts that had prekindergarten or summer preschool programs prior to House Bill 72 have been the most enthusiastic.

The reactions of districts to these preschools illustrate the problems of instituting new programs in the schools. Even under the best of conditions, unfamiliarity and novelty present some problems; if, in addition, there is suspicion or even hostility--as there is in the case of preschool programs, which some educators consider "child rearing" or "day care" rather than education--then the difficulties are compounded. Of course, the current conditions are not the best: the rush of implementing House Bill 72, the press of other requirements, classroom shortages, and uncertainty about state funding have made the past year extremely difficult for districts.   In this situation, the lack of any technical assistance from TEA or any other statewide organization is especially serious.

The future problems facing the preschool programs are those of quality and access. The lack of required transportation is one barrier. Another is that these programs have not been designed with the needs of working parents in mind.   Children with working mothers--who include the majority of low-income children eligible for the prekindergarten--may not be able to attend prekindergarten unless these programs are coordinated with afterschool care.

The issues of quality merit the closest attention. The exemplary programs that have created a public consciousness about the benefits of early childhood education--especially Head Start and the Perry Preschool--are programs of high quality, low pupil/teacher ratios, and staff well trained in early childhood. Compared to these programs, the pupil/teacher ratios in the prekindergarten and summer preschool programs are much too high, and the requirements for training appropriate for teachers of young children are weak. The quality of these programs needs to be improved, by reducing teacher/pupil ratios, improving training, and providing technical assistance by individuals with expertise and experience in early childhood education. Unless this is done, there is little chance that the preschool programs legislated by House Bill 72 will have the same success in preparing disadvantaged children for school as the exemplary programs on which they are based.

Appendix

MODEL PRESCHOOL PROGRAMS IN TEXAS

Prior to House Bill 72, very few districts provided prekindergarten programs. A few districts did have such programs, however, and the reasons for their existence are illuminating.

FORT WORTH I.S.D.

Fort Worth ISD has provided a prekindergarten program since the early 1970s. The underlying philosophy of the program is that an effective prekindergarten program prevents costs which would be incurred later in the form of remedial education: "Research has shown that when a high quality preschool is provided, disadvantaged children increase their chances of higher academic performance, lower delinquency rates and better earning prospects."[43]

The Fort Worth prekindergarten program is actually a continuation of a federally funded program for disadvantaged children called the Center Cities Project, which ran from 1968 through 1971. A grant of $1.5 million for a period of three years was awarded competitively to each of twenty-six cities across the nation. Children aged two through five from low-income families were eligible. The success of the Center Cities Project, as well as the enthusiasm of the staff and aides who remained once the project was through, led to the development of the current prekindergarten program, which is funded by federal Title I (now Chapter 1) revenues.

The typical classroom has twenty-two students, one teacher, and an aide, making the pupil/teacher ratio 11:1. However, the district has experimented with "differentiated staffing." Some classes have as many as thirty-three students, with one teacher and two aides. In another pattern, one teacher supervises two or more classrooms of twenty-two students each, with the assistance of two aides per classroom. Other patterns include one teacher and three aides for forty-four students and one teacher and four aides for fifty-five students. A comparison of educational attainment indicated the program with one teacher supervising two or more classrooms with two aides in each classroom of twenty-two students was as effective as the "traditional" pattern of one teacher, one aide, and twenty-two students.[44] These variations have been used in the district for about ten years, primarily to improve cost effectiveness and to remedy teacher shortages.[45]

To facilitate accessibility, the program has been placed in schools with large populations of students receiving free or reduced-price lunches. Eligibility is also based on age and the score attained on the Preschool Screening Evaluation test. Auditory, visual, motor, and language skills are emphasized during the six-hour program.

Upon completion of the program, children are given a second Preschool Screening Evaluation test. Individual improvement is determined by a comparison of the pretest and posttest. According to a 1983-84 "Administrative Summary" of the program, "The prekindergarten students attained on the average, 90% of the program objectives." The mean pretest score was four and the mean posttest score was nine out of the ten items measured."[46]

Approximately 1,694 four-year-olds were served during the 1983-84 school year. The cost per child was about $1,537. However, this figure must be interpreted with care: it includes staffing costs and some materials, but does not include administrators, space, utilities, or other indirect costs. Since expenditures on teachers in Texas tend to be about half of total expenditures per pupil, the $1,537 figure is probably a serious underestimate of full cost.

Another exemplary feature of the Fort Worth Program is the provision of afterschool child care for children with working parents. Two nonprofit organizations, Clayton Child Care, Inc., and the YWCA, both provide services in school district classrooms.

AUSTIN ISD

The Austin early childhood program was also started with federal funds for disadvantaged children. It began in 1978, largely at the instigation of elementary administrators and funded by Title I (now Chapter I). The Austin program was recently selected as one of the recipients of the Secretary's Initiative Award to Improve the Quality of Chapter 1 Projects, by the secretary of the Department of Education. The presence of an enthusiastic staff, committed to early childhood education, was central to the success of the program, which in its early days had to persuade other administrators of the value of early childhood education.[47]

The program initially began with a ratio of 10:1, with one teacher and one aide per twenty children. Aides were eliminated because of a reduction in federal funding, so the number of children per classroom was reduced to sixteen. The district estimates its costs to be $1,875 per child, although again this figure includes only teacher salaries and some materials, and is a serious underestimate of full costs.

Although House Bill 72 allows a maximum pupil/teacher ratio of 22:1 for the prekindergarten program, Austin plans to keep its ratio at 16:1. The district administration believes that the 22:1 ratio is too high and does not wish to compromise the quality of its program. Because of this lower ratio and an absence of empty classrooms, not all children eligible for preschool services under the law will be allowed to participate in the Austin program. However, the district hopes eventually to triple its program under House Bill 72.

Currently, the district has twenty-five prekindergarten classrooms; fifteen of the classes include Chapter 1 eligible children, six are bilingual, and four are migrant. Two students in each of the bilingual classrooms are non-LEP. The district estimates that approximately 1,200 children are eligible under House Bill 72 and will have to build an additional fifty classrooms to serve them all.

Another exemplary feature of the program is that it runs for the full school day, from 8 a.m. to 2:30 p.m. A number of organizations such as Extend-a-Care, community schools, the Department of Parks and Recreation, and the district itself provide afterschool child care in the schools, making it easy for children with working parents to enroll in the program.

HOUSTON ISD

Houston ISD was chosen as an exemplary district because its prekindergarten program for the fall of 1985 is particularly well planned and detailed. Approximately 9,000 preschool children will qualify for the program: 4,200 will qualify under the free lunch program, and 4,800 will qualify as LEP. The cost per classroom was determined to be approximately $2,400. The district will offer a half-day, full-year program. A morning and afternoon session will provide parents with a choice of the most convenient time.

To identify its eligible population, a questionnaire was mailed to all parents in April, to describe the program, inform parents of the eligibility requirements, and determine the number of students per campus. During May, all potential children were screened to determine language proficiency, and document eligibility and to confer with the parents. Enrollment will take place in August.

Like other districts, Houston faces the problems of financing, teachers, and classrooms. Different portions of the prekindergarten program will be funded by various sources, depending upon the makeup of the preschool population. The state bilingual allotment, state compensatory education, the Emergency Immigration Act, Transition Program for Refugee Children, and the HISD general fund are all potential sources of funding.

Approximately 210 teachers are needed for the program. Potential sources include teachers employed with HISD who already have a kindergarten endorsement, Head Start teachers, and private day care center teachers. In addition, state compensatory education funds may be used to finance the retraining of those elementary teachers on staff interested in teaching prekindergarten. Local agencies and schools will also be notified of available positions.

All district campuses were surveyed to determine the facilities available for the program. The campus facilities chosen to provide the program are within walking distance of most eligible children; therefore, transportation will not be provided.

THE FORT WORTH SUMMER PRESCHOOL PROGRAM

Since 1973, Fort Worth ISD has offered a four-week, three-hour summer program for four-year-olds. Children who lived in Chapter I attendance areas, were four years old by September 1, and had a score of seven or less on a test called the Preschool Screening Evaluation were eligible for the program. The purpose of the program was to enhance the learning experiences of the children as measured by a higher score on the Preschool Screening Evaluation posttest.[48] In addition, the children were immunized and screened to prepare them for the regular school year.

To comply with the House Bill 72 preschool summer school requirement, Fort Worth ISD will offer a separate summer program for those children who are eligible under the new state requirements.[49] All children who qualify for bilingual education will be placed in the eight-week state-mandated program. Although the district has typically maintained a pupil/teacher ratio of 11:1 for its summer programs, the 18:1 ratio prescribed by the legislature will be used in the eight-week program due to cost factors.

THE BRAZOSPORT SUMMER BILINGUAL PROGRAM

Approximately two years ago, Brazosport began a half-day, three-week summer bilingual program for children in kindergarten through grade two.   The purpose of the summer bilingual education program was to improve oral communication and language development skills. The program included students in need of remedial services, as determined by teachers who nominated them for the program. This program will be expanded to serve the population required by House Bill 72.   The pupil/teacher ratio of 15:1 previously used in the summer program will remain, even though a ratio of 18:1 is permitted. Brazosport administrators believe that even the 15:1 ratio is probably too high.[50]

Notes

[1]On the history of early childhood efforts, see Marvin Lazerson, "The Historical Antecedents of Early Childhood Education," National Society for the Study of Education, Seventy-first Yearbook, Early Childhood Education (Chicago: University of Chicago Press, 1972).

[2]House Bill 240, (61st Legislature, 1969) required public schools to provide kindergarten programs for the "educationally handicapped," defined as:

1. A child who could not speak, read, or comprehend the English language, or
2. A child who was from a family whose income, according to standards promulgated by the State Board of Education, was at or below subsistence level. [Texas H.B. 240, 61st Leg., 1969]

It is interesting to note that this language is very similar to that of the House Bill 72 prekindergarten program, which also targets special populations.

[3]Interview with Dr. Yvonne Katz, Associate Commissioner for General Education, Texas Education Agency, Austin, Texas, March 22, 1985.

[4]Larry Schweinhart, "Early Childhood Programs in the 1980s," High/Scope Educational Research Foundation, Ypsilanti, Michigan, December 11, 1984.

[5]Texas H.B. 612, 56th Leg. (1959).

[6]Texas Education Agency, Biennial Report 1970-72 (Austin, Texas, 1973), 43.

[7]Ibid.

[8]Texas S.B. 230, 61st Leg. (1969).

[9]Interview with Dr. Elizabeth MacNaughton, SCOPE Committee Member, Houston, Texas, October 19, 1984.

[10]On Head Start, see Irving Lazar et al., The Persistence of Preschool Effects: A Long-Term Follow-up of Fourteen Infant and Preschool Experiments (Washington, D.C.: Department of Health, Education and Welfare, October 1977); on the Perry Preschool, see John Berrueta-Clement et al., Changed Lives: The Effects of the Perry Preschool Program on Youths through Age 19, Monographs of the High/Scope Educational Research Foundation, no. 8 (Ypsilanti, Mich.:

High/Scope Press, 1984).

[11]Interview with Carlos Gregory, Personnel Administrator, Brownsville ISD, Brownsville, Texas, April 17, 1985.

[12]Interview with K. Allen Johnson, Associate Superintendent for Instruction, El Paso ISD, El Paso, Texas, April 22, 1985.

[13]Interview with Dr. Timy Baranoff, Assistant Superintendent for Elementary Education, Austin ISD, Austin, Texas, February 11, 1985.

[14]Interview with Tony Rico, Superintendent, Weslaco ISD, Weslaco, Texas, April 18, 1985.

[15]Houston Independent School District, "Houston I.S.D. Issues, Concerns and Solutions Related to House Bill 72," Houston, Texas, 1984, 5.

[16]Ibid., exhibit C.

[17]Ibid., 5.

[18]Interview with Dr. Preston Stephens, Superintendent of Schools, La Vernia ISD, La Vernia, Texas, April 12, 1985.

[19]Interview with Dr. Yvonne Katz, Associate Commissioner for General Education, Texas Education Agency, Austin, Texas, March 22, 1985.

[20]U.S. Department of Health, Education and Welfare, Federal Programs For Young Children: Review and Recommendations, vol. II, Review of Evaluation Data for Federally Sponsored Projects For Children, by Sheldon H. White et al. (Cambridge, Mass.: Huron Institute, September 15, 1972), 189.

[21]L. J. Schweinhart and D. P. Weikart, Young Children Grow Up: The Effects of the Perry Preschool Program on Youths through Age 15, Monographs of the High/Scope Educational Research Foundation no. 7 (Ypsilanti, Mich.: High/Scope Press, 1980), 17.

[22]Berrueta-Clement et al., Changed Lives, 101.

[23]Schweinhart and Weikart, Young Children Grow Up, 22.

[24]Personal communication, Lawrence Schweinhart, February 16, 1985.

[25]Edward Zigler and Jeanette Valentine, Project Head Start (New York: Free Press, 1979), 5.

[26]Ibid., 125-6.

[27]Abt Associates, Children at the Center, Final Report of the National Day Care Study (Cambridge: Abt Associates, March 1979).

[28]Interview with Anita Uphaus, Early Childhood Coordinator, Chapter 1 Prekindergarten, Austin ISD, Austin, Texas, April 25, 1985; interview with John Barnett, Director of Staff Development, Fort Worth ISD, Fort Worth, Texas, April 8, 1985.

[29]Interview with Catherine Cooper, Associate Professor and Head, Child Development and Family Relationships, University of Texas at Austin, Austin, Texas, May 13, 1985.

[30]Interview with Barbara Dale, Assistant Superintendent for Curriculum, Taylor ISD, Taylor, Texas, March 19, 1985.

[31]Interview with Dr. Timy Baranoff, Director of Curriculum, Austin, ISD, Austin, Texas, February 11, 1985.

[32]U.S. Department of Commerce, Bureau of the Census, 1980 General Social and Economic Characteristics of Texas: Population (Washington, D.C.: U.S. Government Printing Office, 1983), table 67, 45-114.

[33]Interview with Ramon Magallanes, Education Program Director, Division of Bilingual Education, Texas Education Agency, Austin, Texas, April 19, 1985.

[34]Texas H.B. 51, 56th Leg. (1959).

[35]Texas Education Agency, 43rd Biennial Report 1962-1964 (Austin, Texas, 1965), 30.

[36]Texas Education Agency, 48th Biennial Report 1972-1974, (Austin, Texas, 1975), 49.

[37]Houston ISD, "Houston I.S.D.," 5.

[38]Interview with Oscar Cardenas, Director, Office of Bilingual Education, Texas Education Agency, June 25, 1985.

[39]Interview with Tony Rico, April 18, 1985.

[40]Interview with Jay Caperton, Director of Staff Development and Technology, Brazosport ISD, Lake Jackson, Texas, April 23, 1985.

[41]Interview with Dr. Bill Borgers, Superintendent, Taylor ISD, Taylor, Texas, November 15, 1984.

[42]Interview with Tony Rico, April 18, 1985.

[43]Fort Worth Independent School District, "Prekindergarten Program 1983-84," Fort Worth, Texas, October 1984, 1.

[44]Ibid., 3-4.

[45]Interview with Anna Perez, Program Manager, Fort Worth ISD, Fort Worth, Texas, March 29, 1985.

[46]Fort Worth Independent School District, "Administrative Summary, Prekindergarten Program 1983-84," Fort Worth, Texas, October 1984.

[47]Interview with Dr. Timy Baranoff, February 11, 1985.

[48]Fort Worth ISD, "Early Childhood Summer Roundup 1984," Fort Worth, Texas, October 1984.

[49]Interview with Alice Contreras, Director of Bilingual Education, Fort Worth ISD, Fort Worth, Texas, April 9, 1985.

[50]Interview with Jay Caperton, April 23, 1985.

CHAPTER NINE
BLAME IT ON 72:
HOUSE BILL 246 AND CURRICULUM REFORMS IN TEXAS

The implementation of House Bill 72 has been a complicated and often confusing task for hundreds of school districts in Texas. The bill has inundated administrators and teachers with information from a variety of sources including the legislature, the governor, the Texas Education Agency, and numerous professional associations, which have all attempted to guide school personnel through the maze of provisions. These difficulties have been compounded by the requirements of a very different bill, House Bill 246, which reformed the curriculum in Texas schools beginning in 1984-85.

Because of the statewide implementation of the new curriculum requirements in the midst of the House Bill 72 uproar, confusion has been widespread. House Bill 72 and its sponsors have been blamed for a number of provisions required by House Bill 246. School administrators, teachers, and the public have had trouble distinguishing the two bills. Therefore, it is necessary to examine House Bill 246 in order to understand its distinctiveness and its implications for House Bill 72.

Several provisions in House Bill 246 and in the related curriculum rules promulgated by the State Board of Education were repeated and clarified in provisions of House Bill 72. Both reform initiatives contain a requirement for a passing grade minimum of 70 percent.[1] House Bill 246 required that district school boards institute policies "designed to prevent distractions from interruptions and loss of scheduled class time by any activity during the school day"; House Bill 72 took this provision one step further by requiring the State Board of Education to limit participation in extracurricular activities during the school day;[2] and by requiring that school boards adopt policies limiting interruptions during the school day for nonacademic activities.[3] Another provision established in House Bill 246 and expanded in House Bill 72 is the requirement to develop promotion and retention policies based on academic achievement and mastery of essential elements; as expressed in House Bill 72, "A district may not grant social promotion."[4] The similarities in these bills, along with the initial implementation of both in 1984-85, have caused much of the confusion over House Bill 72 and House Bill 246. However, many provisions of the two bills differ, and the two should be viewed as separate educational reforms.

Although the simultaneous implemention of House Bill 72 and House Bill 246 has caused difficulty and confusion, the problems analyzed in this chapter should not be interpreted as criticisms of the curriculum reforms themselves. Most teachers and administrators support the curriculum changes and feel that over the long run they will increase standards, restore some coherence to the curriculum, and improve the quality of instruction.

THE PROVISIONS OF HOUSE BILL 246

The curriculum reform bill, passed in 1981, resulted from two years of study of statewide curriculum standards. In 1979, the 66th Texas Legislature directed the State Board of Education to undertake a statewide study of curriculum for Texas public schools, because of a concern that the state's curriculum requirements had become fragmented and that the "basics" of education were being slighted because of public school attempts to address too many nonacademic goals. As the resolution creating the study declared, "The current requirements do not represent a truly comprehensive and systematic set of curriculum elements which are mandates for each school district and which are realistic in terms of expectations of society."[5] The resolution directed the State Board to produce a realistic and relevant statement of elements to be included in a well-balanced curriculum, formulated around a core curriculum including English language arts, mathematics, science, social studies, and computer science. In retrospect, this resolution was an early manifestation of the concerns with academic education and the core curriculum that burst forth in 1983 in many national reports.

A Curriculum Study Panel consisting of members of SBOE, the Texas Senate and House of Representatives, and the Governor's Advisory Committee on Education submitted a series of recommendations to the 67th Legislature in November of 1980. In 1981, the legislature passed House Bill 246, which embodied a number of recommendations from the Curriculum Study Panel. The bill repealed twenty separate existing laws concerning public school curriculum and specified the twelve subject areas that comprise a well-balanced curriculum.[6] The required subject areas exceed the "basics," because groups representing other areas of study convinced the legislature that their subjects should be included in a well-balanced curriculum.

The twelve designated subject areas are:

1. English language arts;
2. Other languages, to the extent possible;
3. Mathematics;
4. Science;
5. Health;
6. Physical education;
7. Fine arts;
8. Social studies;
9. Economics, with an emphasis on the free enterprise system and its benefits;
10. Business education;
11. Vocational education; and
12. Texas and United States history as individual subjects and in reading courses.[7]

The bill delegated to the State Board of Education the responsibility for designating the "essential elements" of each subject area and the authority to require each district to provide instruction in those essential elements at appropriate grade levels.

After a year of study, public hearings, and local district workshops, the Texas Education Agency presented a plan for curriculum revision to the State Board. In March 1984, the State Board adopted the final proposal for the new curriculum, which is codified in Chapter 75 of the Texas Administrative Code.[8] The rules outline the essential elements of each subject area, specify the amount of time in each day which must be devoted to each subject, set high school graduation requirements, describe acceptable options for offering courses, and require school districts to develop district policy on promotion, retention, remediation, and placement. The new requirements are being phased in during 1984-85 and 1985-86.

All provisions concerning instructional time required in each subject area for grades kindergarten through six must be fully implemented in the 1984-85 school year. Implementation of the essential elements began in the 1984-85 school year and will be completed by the 1985-86 school year. The secondary curriculum requirements, including the teaching of essential elements, must be implemented in the 1985-86 school year. All students entering the ninth grade in the 1984-85 school year and thereafter are required to meet the graduation requirements outlined in Chapter 75. The school districts' policies for promotion, retention, remediation, and placement will be enacted at the beginning of the 1985-86 school year.[9]

The "essential elements" have been referred to as "the heart of House Bill 246."[10] An element is a brief statement of a specific skill or concept within a subject. There are thousands of these elements in each subject, and the more elements a student masters, the better he or she understands the subject. Subject elements are set out in a sequence that describes a step-by-step learning process of increasingly complex concepts and skills.

There is simply not enough time in the school day to teach all elements well, because there are potentially so many in each subject area. Therefore, the legislature directed the State Board to define the most important or "essential" curriculum elements by grade level for each of the twelve selected subject areas. The essential elements set the priorities for the curriculum by determining what students should learn. Two statewide groups of educators and interested citizens developed and approved the essential elements to be taught in the Texas public schools. Subsequent public hearings throughout the state enabled parents, teachers, and others to express their views on the composition of the required curriculum. The result is a basic curriculum for all public schools in Texas.

Mastery learning is another educational concept introduced in the curriculum revision effort. Mastery learning models are based on the assumption that almost all students can learn what schools have to teach them, provided the learning time and the instructional process are altered in accordance with the students' level of performance.[11] This approach requires that teachers ascertain whether students have mastered a particular skill or area of knowledge before moving to new skills or materials. By implementing a mastery learning model, educators in a district would fulfill at least three basic requirements of House Bill 246: teaching for mastery, monitoring student progress, and reteaching students who have not mastered some essential elements. Ideally, meeting these three requirements would lead to the elimination of social promotion, which is also a goal of House Bill 72.

The State Board of Education rules for House Bill 246 require school districts to develop procedures for evaluating the effectiveness of the schools' instructional programs. This process must include an annual review of data compiled by the teachers regarding student progress in the essential elements. The board must direct administrators and ensure adequate preparation time for teachers and must adopt policies to prevent interruptions and loss of class time due to any activity.[12]

Still another new responsibility of school boards is to develop policies for promotion, retention, remediation, and appropriate placement of students based on specific criteria, including the mastery of the essential elements.[13] This provision and the 70 percent minimum passing grade requirement have forced districts to develop alternatives to past promotion and retention practices.[14] The required policies must also cover methods for reteaching students who do not achieve mastery of the essential elements; in order to determine whether students demonstrate mastery of essential elements, H.B. 246 requires that districts develop tests or other ways to measure mastery. The hope is that these policies will reduce retention, reduce the need for remediation, and increase overall student achievement.[15]

Finally, graduation requirements were upgraded by House Bill 246. Over the past few years, there has been a significant movement at the college level to upgrade admission requirements; as part of this trend, the University of Texas and Texas A&M recently raised their admissions standards. The State Board of Education kept these changes in mind when developing new graduation requirements in House Bill 246.[16] The Rules for Curriculum now require that all students complete a minimum of 21 units of credit to receive a high school diploma.[17] A one-semester course is typically half a unit; with a typical load of five to six courses at a time a student can accumulate the required 21 units in three and a half to four years. The required units must include the following:

1. English language arts - 4 units;
2. Mathematics - 3 units;
3. Science - 2 units;
4. Social studies sciences - 2 and 1/2 units;
5. Economics - 1/2 unit;
6. Physical education - 1 and 1/2 units;
7. Health education - 1/2 unit;
8. Electives - 7 units.

LOCAL REACTIONS TO THE CURRICULUM REFORMS

In our interviews in school districts, we found little opposition to the concept of a statewide curriculum. Most administrators and teachers feel the new curriculum requirements are an effective way of improving the educational system. The frustration and confusion expressed at the local level have been the result of problems experienced while implementing rules for House Bill 246, rather than the result of philosophical differences with the legislation's intent.

Prior to House Bill 246, there were wide disparities among districts in the curricula being offered. In many instances, district interests and the local economy influenced the curriculum direction. These differences were particularly apparent in vocational education programs. Many of the wealthier districts had computer science programs in place several years before House Bill 246 required such courses, and they also tended to have elaborate elective course offerings which poorer districts could not afford. Grading systems, graduation requirements, and reporting systems also varied among districts; districts often had a difficult time integrating transfer students into their schools.

Because of this variation, the requirements of Chapter 75 have affected some districts much more than others. The districts in the state which were offering the required courses and credits before the passage of H.B. 246 have had little difficulty implementing the new requirements. However, other districts had a curriculum which could only be described as the "bare bones minimum." Those districts have faced the need to redesign their curricula and to absorb the costs of providing additional teachers, courses, and facilities in order to meet the requirements. The state's poorer districts have had the greatest difficulty meeting the mandate for upgraded curricula. Chapter 75 does provide districts the opportunity to apply for hardship status if they are unable to comply with the requirements by the designated deadline.[18] However, only three districts have applied to the commissioner of education for hardship status, and these have asked for a temporary extension of the deadline.[19] School districts have worked diligently to comply with Chapter 75 by the deadline.

Despite this progress, many implementation problems have been experienced in the school districts of Texas, regardless of size or wealth. A number of provisions in H.B. 246 and Chapter 75 require additional expenditures, yet the curriculum legislation does not provide funding to meet these costs. Most districts have faced the initial costs of developing or revising district curriculum guides to reflect the changes in the requirements and to include the essential elements of each course offering. Many schools paid their teachers and other staff throughout the summer to write the curriculum guides, while other schools contracted with curriculum consultants to complete the task. The printing and paper costs alone were substantial for some of the larger districts.

Furthermore, many districts are faced with the costs of hiring additional teachers in order to offer the required courses. The requirement of an additional year of math and science has exacerbated the already severe shortages in these fields. Additional requirements in English, reading, foreign language, and elementary fine arts, social studies, and physical education have forced most districts to hire a number of new teachers.

The computer literacy requirement has generated additional costs for new classrooms, necessary hardware, and teaching materials, and the additional credit of laboratory science has forced districts to provide additional laboratory facilities.

Administrators in most districts have assumed that the funding provisions in House Bill 72 would provide the additional state aid necessary to meet the curriculum mandates. However, this was not true for the majority of districts, and House Bill 72 has other requirements of its own. Because the provisions in House Bill 246 required additional expenditures for personnel, facilities, and instructional resources, and because House Bill 72 provided additional state funds to many school districts, confusion between the two bills seemed inevitable. It has sometimes been said that in practice House Bill 72 has funded the requirements of House Bill 246, but that was never the intent of the state aid increases under House Bill 72.

One particular source of revenue in House Bill 72 that has frequently been used to cover the curriculum requirements of House Bill 246 is the allotment for compensatory education.[20] These funds can be used to cover any costs of remediation, including remedial programs, afterschool tutorials, and other programs a district chooses to define as remedial in nature (including reteaching those students who have not demonstrated mastery of some essential elements). When state compensatory education revenues are used to support these programs, other funds at the local level become available to cover some of the additional costs of curriculum requirements.[21]

Although the poorer districts in the state receive substantial increases in state aid through House Bill 72, these districts will be stretching these funds to cover the requirements in both House Bill 72 and House Bill 246. In years to come state aid to many districts will actually decrease (as explained in chapter 1), yet these districts will still be required to meet the same mandates. There is no funding provision in House Bill 72 for the construction of new facilities, although many districts have been forced to undertake construction in order to provide adequate classroom space for the expanded curriculum requirements in House Bill 246 and the lower pupil/teacher ratio at the elementary level in House Bill 72. As a result of inadequate state funding levels, many districts have relied on local funds to put the new requirements into place--but reliance on local revenues places a greater hardship on poor districts.

Alternative delivery procedures outlined in Chapter 75 have somewhat alleviated the financial and administrative burdens of providing the new curriculum offerings.[22] The options available to districts include:

1. Cooperatives--two or more districts arranging for the cooperative use of personnel, facilities, or materials and equipment.

2. Contracting--districts contracting for the delivery of instruction with other districts or approved institutions.

3. Technology--districts utilizing a variety of technological advancements including computer-assisted instruction, interactive television, and video- or audio-taped courses.

4. Adjusted school week--one or more districts delivering instruction within an adjusted school day or school week.

Apart from the fiscal implications, teachers have been affected by various provisions in House Bill 246 and Chapter 75. The shift to mastery learning has been a source of consternation for many teachers, who have had to alter their methods of teaching. The change to the mastery learning concept has been particularly difficult for those experienced teachers who have developed their own individual teaching methodology though the years. Chapter 75, which outlines the essential elements and prescribes how many minutes a day each course must be taught,[23] seems excessively rigid to some teachers, and many have expressed concern that the extensive nature of the essential elements and the prescribed time limits do not allow teachers enough time to implement the new requirements. Teachers are also responsible for keeping track of the students' success in mastering the essential elements and documenting this progress.

An indirect effect of the new curriculum requirements is the displacement of many teachers in elective subject areas. With more courses now being required for graduation, students have less time to take electives. Although most districts are retaining many elective subject areas, the number of classes will be smaller, and fewer teachers will be needed. Many teachers in elective subject areas are being forced to go back to school to seek recertification in other subject areas. This recertification process will take time, although this process may alleviate shortages in some subject areas. However, districts have expressed the concern that some teachers are hesitating to go back to school for recertification.

Teachers blame both House Bill 72 and Chapter 75 for a tremendous increase in the amount of paperwork required. Teachers have to indicate in their lesson plans how each of the essential elements will be taught in their classrooms. They must also document their students' progress toward achieving mastery of the essential elements. Many teachers feel that they are becoming mere clerks, and they dislike spending valuable instructional time and other resources on routine paperwork.[24] John Cole, executive director of the Texas Federation of Teachers, stated that his main concern is the documentation required of teachers to prove they are teaching the essential elements. This problem is magnified at the elementary level, where each teacher is responsible for six to eight subject areas. A number of districts have imposed very complex documentation procedures within their districts-- procedures more detailed and complex than are actually necessary for TEA's accreditation review. However, there are indications that TEA is making an effort to aid districts in developing more reasonable documentation procedures, and there have been a number of legislative proposals to ease the paperwork burden for teachers.[25]

District administrators have experienced as much frustration as teachers in implementing the Chapter 75 curriculum rules, since they give administrators the responsibility for setting local policies. In addition to coping with the anxieties of teachers, administrators have been forced to develop ideas for creative financing of the curriculum requirements. Since the districts were given two years to comply with the curriculum requirements, at the same time that they were coping with the reforms included in House Bill 72, the past two years have been difficult and challenging ones for school administrators.

Most of the administrative difficulties associated with House Bill 246 can be traced to three provisions outlined in Chapter 75. First, school districts are required to provide each student with the opportunity to participate in all courses included in the State Board's description of a well-balanced secondary curriculum. Second, students must be given the opportunity each year to select courses in which they intend to participate from a list that includes all courses constituting a well-balanced curriculum. Third, for those courses where ten or more students indicate that they will participate or courses required for a student to graduate, the district must teach the course.[26] These three provisions require districts to be prepared to offer every course each semester if ten or more students request it. The district must have the resources--teachers, classrooms, and materials--to offer these courses. To meet this requirement, many districts are offering longer school days and have gone to a seven-period day. These solutions not only ease administrative burdens, but they also allow students more class time for taking electives.

Many districts feel that paperwork is a source of frustration for administrators as well as teachers. School principals, counselors, and office staff have been assigned responsibility for keeping track of the documentation prepared by teachers showing teaching of essential elements and progression of students toward mastery. Administrators compile these test results each month along with teacher documentation and present the report to the local school board. Administrators have also shouldered the responsibility for organizing in-service programs to help teachers in the tasks of curriculum writing and teaching of essential elements, responsibilities which have fallen upon the administrators at the local district level.

The regional Education Service Centers have provided assistance to school district administrators in developing ways to implement the curriculum requirements.[27] These centers began operation in 1967 as media centers for area districts, but they have taken on a new importance with the passage of House Bill 72 and House Bill 246. The ESCs are now responsible for coordinating educational services and planning and providing technical assistance to those districts without the resources to meet the requirements on their own. Districts report that the ESCs have been invaluable to local districts during the implementation process.

CONCLUSIONS

Successful implementation of new, complex, controversial legislation requires a clear understanding of the provisions included.   House Bill 72 itself is complex and has proved to be highly controversial. The confusion associated with the provisions in House Bill 246 and Chapter 75 rules have compounded the implementation problems of House Bill 72. The overlapping implementation schedules, some identical provisions, and the reliance on House Bill 72 to provide funding for the House Bill 246 provisions have been the major sources of confusion about the two different reforms. However, the two pieces of legislation are very different, and need to be carefully distinguished in identifying unresolved problems. "Blaming it on House Bill 72" is not an appropriate way to clarify the continuing problems with curriculum reforms and development of appropriate policies.

In retrospect, it would probably have been better to delay   the implementation of House Bill 72 so that the two pieces of legislation did not overlap. However, the difficulties of implementing House Bill 246 and House Bill 72 together should not overshadow the positive aspects of the curriculum reforms. Most teachers and administrators continue to feel that House Bill 246 is a progressive step toward reconstructing a fragmented curriculum and affirming higher standards and that the curriculum reforms are worth pursuing despite the dislocations they may cause.

Notes

[1]Texas Education Agency (TEA), State Board of Education Rules for Curriculum (Austin, 1984), 245.

[2]Texas Education Code, Ch. 21.920(a).

[3]Texas Education Code, Ch. 21.923.

[4]TEA, State Board of Education Rules for Curriculum,: 246; and Texas Education Code, Ch. 21.721(a).

[5]Texas H.C.R. 90, 66th Leg. (1979).

[6]Cheryl Mehl, "Policy Making Abounds with Chapter 75 Rules," Texas Lone Star 2, no. 4 (August 1984): 3.

[7]Texas H. B. 246, 67th Leg. (1981).

[8]Texas House of Representatives, House Study Group, Special Legislative Report, July 16, 1984, Study Paper 104, 17.

[9]TEA, State Board of Education Rules for Curriculum, 241.

[10]Thomas Anderson, Jr., "What Is an Essential Element?" Texas Lone Star 2, no. 4 (August 1984): 1. The discussion of essential elements in this chapter was taken from this publication.

[11]Roberto Zamora, "Mastery Learning Makes Difference," Texas Lone Star 2, no. 4 (Aug. 1984): 7.

[12]TEA, State Board of Education Rules for Curriculum, 2-3.

[13]Texas Education Code, Ch. 75.141, .142, .151, and .170.

[14]TEA, State Board of Education Rules for Curriculum, 245; and Texas Education Code, Ch. 21.721.

[15]Edward Manigold, "Promotion, Retention Policy Demands Several Considerations," Texas Lone Star 2, no. 4 (August 1984): 4.

[16]Texas State Board of Education, "A Nation at Risk: How Texas Stacks Up," included in Comptroller of Public Accounts, Education Workpapers I (Austin, 1984), 3-4.

[17]19 Texas Administrative Code, Ch. 75.171.

[18]TEA, State Board of Education Rules for Curriculum, 246.

[19]Interview with Dr. Iva Nell Turman, Director of Special Programs, Texas Education Agency, Austin, Texas, February 22, 1985.

[20]Interview with Sally Haenelt, Committee Clerk, Texas Senate Education Committee, Austin, Texas, October 23, 1984.

[21]Interview with Sandra Lennox, Staff Services Assistant, Texas Education Agency, October 22, 1984.

[22]TEA, State Board of Education Rules for Curriculum, 246.

[23]Ibid., 243.

[24]Interview with John Cole, Executive Director, Texas Federation of Teachers, Austin, Texas, October 22, 1984.

[25]Interview with Johnny Veselka, Assistant Executive Director, Texas Association of School Administrators, Austin, Texas, October 23, 1984.

[26]TEA, Board of Education Rules for Curriculum, 232.

[27]Manigold, "Promotions," 4.

CHAPTER TEN
CONCLUSIONS AND RECOMMENDATIONS

The recent school reform legislation is an attempt by the legislature to help Texas schools achieve two goals: improving educational quality and furthering educational equity, particularly by narrowing the disparities between rich and poor districts and by increasing funding for compensatory, bilingual, and special education.

Most of the educators we interviewed seemed to think that many of the new state requirements, although occasionally burdensome, were necessary and have produced desirable changes at the local level. The state has been successful in communicating the message that academic and teaching standards must be given higher priority. Most educators also agreed that the additional funding received by most districts has been valuable in increasing the salaries of teachers, in meeting many of the state requirements in House Bill 72 (and House Bill 246), and in equalizing resources between rich and poor districts. Indeed, the positive attitudes towards House Bill 72 were striking, especially given the burdens that the legislation placed on administrators to respond quickly and the controversies that have been generated by several provisions.

However, local administrators expressed concern that, over the long run, state funding levels may be inadequate to pay for many of the state requirements. If funding indeed turns out to be inadequate, this will have adverse effects on both educational quality and equity in Texas. The adverse effects on equity will occur because wealthy districts are better able to supplement state funding with local revenues. Educational quality will suffer in those districts where local revenues are insufficient to pay for reforms not adequately funded by the state. In addition, the effectiveness of some provisions of House Bill 72 is unclear, and more thorough analysis of their consequences over the next several years is necessary. In this conclusion we offer recommendations for continued monitoring of the aspects of House Bill 72 which are potentially the most troublesome.

STATE MECHANISMS FOR PROMOTING EDUCATIONAL QUALITY AND EXCELLENCE

The state has three basic mechanisms by which it can influence educational policy. The first is prescription: the state may simply require that districts follow a particular practice. Prescription is most likely to be used when state legislators or the public call for the definition and maintenance of standards. Examples of state-prescribed standards in House Bill 72 and House Bill 246 are rules about extracurricular activities, curriculum content requirements, high school graduation requirements, and the career ladder.

Prescriptive methods have the advantage of enabling the state to compel cooperation from reluctant or recalcitrant districts. As we found in our interviews with school administrators, local districts may also implement changes more rapidly when they perceive that those changes are required and enforced by the state. However, state prescriptions have the disadvantage of infringing on local control; they may reduce the flexibility of school districts to develop solutions appropriate to local conditions and may generate resentment if educators feel that they are not able to run their schools the way they see fit. House Bill 246's detailed requirements for the amount of time to be devoted to specific subjects are examples of how state prescriptions can reduce local flexibility.

Another state mechanism is financial assistance to districts. House Bill 72 increased financial assistance to Texas districts by over $900 million. Most of this was general aid to help poor districts increase their expenditures. Some of the additional aid, however, was designated for specific purposes, such as compensatory education, bilingual education, and the development of the career ladder.

The principal purposes of the increased aid in House Bill 72 were to increase teacher salaries and to promote equity among poor and rich districts. Financial assistance is likely to promote excellence by enabling districts to implement changes, such as the state-required reduction of pupil/teacher ratios, that they would be unable to afford out of local revenues.

Technical assistance to local districts is the third mechanism available to the state to improve education. Technical assistance includes the provision of information about how to improve education; it can take the form of workshops to train teachers and administrators or on-site consulting by state personnel expert in a given subject. A special category of technical assistance is dissemination, in which the state informs districts how other school systems in similar circumstances have handled a particular problem effectively and identifies model programs within the state or in other states. Dissemination can be more effective than other means of technical assistance, for two reasons. First, teachers and administrators may be more receptive to knowledge transmitted by their peers. Second, the process of identifying effective programs and districts can spur local effort by providing public recognition for success.

Technical assistance is an indispensable complement to state funding and prescription, because local teachers and administrators may lack information about how to carry out reforms effectively. For example, our survey found wide disparities in knowledge of how to implement the state-mandated career ladder and almost no familiarity with preschool programs. The state provides most of its technical assistance through the twenty Educational Service Centers.

Of these three state mechanisms--prescription, financial assistance, and technical assistance--House Bill 72 and House Bill 246 provided both prescription and financial assistance. However, there was little attention devoted in either bill to technical assistance or dissemination, and House Bill 72 provided no additional funding for the Education Service Centers. In fact, base funding for the Education Service Centers will be cut about 5 percent in 1985-86 and 1986-87, from the $7.7 million in House Bill 72 to $7.3 million, and the categorical aid to the Service Centers of $1 per pupil has stayed the same for many years despite continued inflation.[1] Given the agency's extensive list of other responsibilities, TEA is unlikely to devote adequate attention to technical assistance and dissemination activities unless additional state funding is provided explicitly for them. This is one of the major gaps in the reform legislation that future sessions of the legislature should address.

In addition, the balance between prescription and financial assistance needs further attention, for two reasons. First, the current practice of requiring educational changes without funding such changes explicitly sometimes leads districts to resist these reforms. Such requirements also place relatively heavier burdens on low-wealth districts, creating possibilities for new inequities in education reforms.

Second, we fear that reliance on prescription in House Bill 72 and House Bill 246 may have gone too far in diluting local control. In some districts we observed a dependence on the Texas Education Agency and the State Board of Education to clarify requirements of House Bill 72--rather than local initiatives to interpret legislation according to local conditions and sound educational practice. If necessary, the state may have to consider strengthening local ability to make educational policy, through technical assistance and strengthening of schools of education, but the legislature and the State Board should at the very least take care not to erode any further the capacities and initiative of local educators.

MONITORING EQUALIZATION AND THE ABILITY OF DISTRICTS TO PAY FOR REFORMS

As chapter 1 indicated, House Bill 72 contained several mechanisms for equalizing revenues between rich and poor districts. However, while differences in spending have been narrowed in 1984-85, substantial inequalities still remain. The equalizing power of House Bill 72 will unfortunately grow weaker in the next few years, because state aid will be roughly constant (or even declining) in a period of continuing inflation. We conclude that the equalization problem may become more serious over the next few years and that policymakers need to monitor spending disparities carefully.

Another kind of spending problem arises because of mismatch between the financial assistance and the prescriptions of House Bill 72. Most of these prescriptions were not specifically funded, even though they require districts to spend more on specific purposes; for example, the maximum class size of twenty-two in kindergarten through grade two requires some districts to hire more teachers and build new classrooms, expenses that are not specifically budgeted in House Bill 72. Many districts have therefore used increases in general-purpose state aid to cover the new requirements.

Because the expense of carrying out many of the new state mandates is likely to be high, the increases in costs to districts over time may well exceed the additional funding made available under House Bill 72. If this is true in poor districts as well as wealthy districts, we are likely to see wealth differences produce wide disparities in the ability of districts to carry out the legislative requirements of House Bill 72.

Consequently, the legislature and citizens interested in the quality of education in Texas need to monitor this potential problem. For example, the proportion of failing students attending tutorials, the pupil/teacher ratio in them, and evidence of their effectiveness can be used to indicate whether districts are successfully able to provide afterschool help to students who are doing poorly in school. Likewise, researchers should monitor pupil/teacher ratios in prekindergarten programs and other measures of quality and compare the number of children served by those programs with estimates of the size of the eligible population.

In addition, policymakers and interested citizens should monitor the following indicators of progress toward equal opportunity in education:

- <u>Relative per Pupil Spending among Districts:</u> As chapter 1 of this report pointed out, the effects of House Bill 72 in equalizing per pupil expenditures between districts have been small, and these disparities may widen as the equalizing power of House Bill 72 grows weaker. The state should continue to monitor expenditure patterns carefully to see whether further equalization efforts are warranted.

- <u>Relative Abilities of Rich and Poor Districts to Attract Qualified Teacher Applicants:</u> Our study found that some districts are able to pick and choose among a wide variety of qualified applicants, while other districts feel that they must take the "leftovers." District wealth as well as location plays an important part in districts' ability to choose among a large pool of applicants; the wealthy districts which are willing to pay above-average teacher salaries reported no problems finding qualified teachers for any position they wanted to fill. Furthermore, while House Bill 72 produces some narrowing in the salary differentials among rich and poor districts, particularly for beginning teachers, these disparities remain substantial. Consequently, ongoing research should monitor the number of applicants per teaching position in districts of varying wealth and location, the precise impact of salary differentials in increasing the size of the applicant pool, and the relative ability and qualifications of newly hired teachers in those districts. Research should also look for indicators of improvement in the ability and qualifications of newly hired teachers in the state's poorer districts. These indicators might include the teachers' high school SAT scores, academic credentials, and previous work experience.

- <u>Average Pupil/Teacher Ratios:</u> While House Bill 72 requires a maximum class size of twenty-two in the early grades, some attention to

class size at the secondary level is also warranted. The experience
of the Austin Independent School District has shown that reduction
in class sizes from twenty-four to fifteen increases achievement in
low-achieving students, although the same class size reductions have
less effect on the academic achievement of average students.[2]
Consequently, differences in average class sizes among districts may
have significant effects on the learning opportunities available to
low-achieving students in different districts.

MEASURES DESIGNED TO IMPROVE THE TEACHING PROFESSION

In attempting to improve educational quality, it is possible to focus
one's effort in several possible ways. One can emphasize improving the quality
and effectiveness of teachers.   Alternatively, one can focus on   the
effectiveness of schools as institutions, on the belief that "the whole is
greater than the sum of the parts" and that a supportive institutional
environment is needed to bring out teachers' best performance. In addition,
one can adopt public policy measures designed to provide additional motivation
to students, and one can train parents to work more effectively with their
children in the home.

House Bill 72 included a number of measures designed to improve the
competency of existing teachers and the skill level of new teachers entering
the profession.   These measures included pay raises for beginning teachers
receiving the state-funded minimum salary; a career ladder to provide
opportunities for more experienced teachers to advance; and competency tests
designed to screen out current and prospective teachers who lack basic skills.
These measures must be evaluated in terms of their effectiveness in serving
one or more of these four functions: recruitment of better people into the
teaching profession; retention of skilled and talented people in   the
profession; exclusion of incompetent or unmotivated teachers; and training of
current and prospective teachers to do their jobs better.

The teacher pay raises may help with recruitment and retention, although
teachers have a long way to go before their salaries are comparable to those
of other professions with comparable skill and training requirements.   In
addition, salary increases for experienced teachers were modest compared to
those for beginning teachers, so the effects of House Bill 72 on retention may
be weaker than its effects on recruitment. The teachers and administrators we
interviewed seemed to think that the effects of the career ladder on
recruitment and retention are likely to be mixed, unless districts receive
assistance in setting up career ladders without creating resentment and
animosity among teachers.   However, comments on the career ladder varied
widely among districts: some appear to have had considerable   success
implementing the career ladder, while others had not even started.

With the enactment of teacher competency testing in House Bill 72, the
state legislature involved itself to an unprecedented degree in the sensitive
issue of how to identify and remove incompetent teachers. The weakness in

this approach is that written tests do a poor job of diagnosing what really needs to be evaluated--the classroom performance of teachers. This fact is recognized by the practitioners of other professions, such as medicine, law, or engineering. Although these fields use written tests to screen individuals entering the profession, lawyers, doctors, and engineers are evaluated almost exclusively by job performance once they begin work. Most of our respondents seemed to think that written tests are almost irrelevant in evaluating classroom performance and that any instrument adequate to examine a teacher's classroom performance will uncover deficiencies in basic skills as well.

Moreover, by enacting the teacher competency test the legislature appears to be saying that the teaching profession is full of incompetent people. If many people perceive this to be the legislature's message, this may reduce public esteem for the teaching profession and undermine the goal of recruiting and retaining better teachers.

The fourth method of improving the teaching profession, developing better training for current and prospective teachers, is an area to which citizens and the legislature need to devote special attention. Much has been said about the need to improve the curricula and academic standards of the state's teacher training programs; this area should be a focus of future reform legislation.

Those concerned with educational reform should consider the following potential measures to improve the teaching profession:

- Prescription: The legislature should conduct a study of how to improve the state standards for schools of teacher education. These institutions should require teacher trainees to take a broader range of academic courses and to participate in more classroom experience earlier in their training. Conceivably, expanding both of these components of teacher education at once will compel teacher education colleges to offer a five-year rather than a four-year program. At the same time, the state can simplify the job of recruiting suitable teachers by making it easier for experienced professionals from other careers to be certified to teach.

- Financial Assistance: Although expanded state assistance has had little success in narrowing the dollar gap between rich and poor districts, state aid has been more successful in raising the overall salary scale of teachers around the state. Continued state assistance will be needed to ensure that the gap between rich and poor districts does not, if anything, become wider in future years. Because rich districts will be able to offer more generous salary supplements to a higher percentage of teachers, the career ladder may add a new dimension to the inequality between rich and poor districts. Adequate state funding for the career ladder in low- and moderate-wealth districts will therefore be essential to prevent this type of inequality from becoming worse.

- Technical Assistance: Although the career ladder requires districts to rate teachers by their classroom proficiency, identifying successful classroom performance is only a part of districts' overall responsibility to help teachers improve their skills. TEA should provide continuous assistance to districts to improve their teacher evaluation, training, and screening programs.

- Dissemination: Because districts have had such widely varying degrees of success in implementing the career ladder, it is especially appropriate for the state to encourage the more successful districts to communicate their methods to everyone else. Consequently, state personnel in charge of monitoring the implementation of the career ladder should also be responsible for identifying these successful districts, and the legislature should be responsible for funding those districts to disseminate information about their methods.

MEASURES DESIGNED TO MAKE SCHOOLS MORE EFFECTIVE

By requiring districts to track student achievement by campus, the performance reports mandated by House Bill 72 will make it possible to identify those schools at which students perform poorly. This gives districts the opportunity to develop programs to improve the performance of such schools.

However, many districts have been aware of their less successful schools for years without developing any systematic program to improve the educational effectiveness of those schools. Consequently, encouraging districts to develop such programs is an appropriate area for state involvement.

The legislature should consider these complementary approaches to school improvement:

- Prescription: The state may require TEA's accreditation visits to examine not only "the quality of learning at each of the district's campuses based on indicators such as scores on achievement tests," as H.B. 72 requires, but also the measures the district is taking to improve academic performance on the poor-performance campuses.

- Financial and Technical Assistance: The legislature should fund the Texas Education Agency to increase its assistance to districts to develop effective school improvement programs.

- Dissemination: The legislature could instruct TEA to identify effective school improvement programs and to disseminate information about those programs around the state. The state should also fund TEA to identify and disseminate effective compensatory, bilingual, and special education projects.

MEASURES TO MOTIVATE AND ASSIST STUDENTS

The student-related reforms in House Bill 246 and House Bill 72 contain two approaches to helping students learn. First, the legislation seeks to motivate students by establishing a clear demarcation between academic success and failure and by making the consequences of failure worse. This is the clear intent of House Bill 72's requirement for numerical grades, designation of a grade below 70 as a failing grade, exclusion of failing students from extracurricular activities, and denial of a high school diploma to students unable to pass all sections of the TEAMS high school exit exam. Second, the legislation requires districts to offer remediation to failing students. With this approach, the legislature hoped to avoid simply driving unsuccessful students out of school.

However, unless the remediation offered is adequate, an increase in dropout rates is precisely what is likely to occur. Our survey found many inadequacies in the tutorial programs designed for remediation. Attendance at tutorials is poor in many districts; in most instances pupil/teacher ratios are too high for meaningful remediation to be taking place; and transportation is frequently not available for students attending tutorials.

The idea of offering remediation to students at the first sign of difficulty in school is a good one, but this remediation is unlikely to be effective in the absence of funding sufficient to reduce pupil/teacher ratios to levels that educational research has shown to be effective--no more than 8:1 or 10:1. Moreover, reformers must recognize that, while the sanctions for failure in House Bill 72 have been put into effect quickly, the development of effective remedial programs, and the adaptation of schools, teachers, and students to the new standards, is a slower process. (Our survey found that a similar delay is occurring in the adoption of the mastery learning techniques required by House Bill 246.)

In the wake of the new reforms, it is especially important for policymakers and citizens to monitor the schools to see whether an increase in student dropout rates is taking place and, if so, what forms of remediation are most effective in preventing dropouts from increasing.

Changes that would help make the student-related provisions of House Bill 72 and House Bill 246 more effective include the following:

- Prescription: The student test data that allow districts to identify the campuses that need assistance also enable districts to evaluate the effectiveness of their state-funded remedial and compensatory education programs. Since evaluation of effectiveness is an important spur to improving programs, the legislature should amend the section on compensatory education to require such evaluations, which districts already must do for their federally funded compensatory education programs. The State Board of Education should direct TEA to monitor how districts use these evaluation results to improve their remedial programs on a campus-by-campus basis.

- <u>Financial Assistance:</u> Admonition that districts reduce pupil/teacher ratios in tutorials are likely to be ineffective in the absence of adequate financial assistance to poor districts to enable them to pay additional teachers to conduct tutorials. Concerned citizens and the legislature need to monitor whether existing state funding for compensatory education is sufficient to support adequate remedial and tutorial programs in poor districts.

- <u>Technical Assistance:</u> Because many teachers find the implementation of mastery learning techniques burdensome, TEA should expand its efforts through the Education Service Centers to help schools develop efficient diagnostic and recording-keeping systems for tracking which students are failing to master the essential elements. In addition, TEA's Division of Compensatory Education should be funded to monitor and offer on-site assistance to teachers and administrators operating state-funded compensatory education projects, just as the division now does with districts' federally funded compensatory education programs.

- <u>Dissemination:</u> Despite the fact that federally funded compensatory education is twenty years old and most school districts have offered remedial programs for failing students for years, districts have not universally mastered the art of <u>successful</u> remediation for failing students. The state can help encourage the dissemination of this art by identifying successful remedial and compensatory programs and by funding those programs' developers to give workshops in different parts of the state as part of the summer workshop programs sponsored by the Education Service Centers.

MEASURES TO PROMOTE PARENT INVOLVEMENT

There is a growing body of evidence to support a belief long held by many educators that parent involvement has a critical influence on student achievement. This should surprise few educators. What is more interesting is the research evidence that programs designed to increase parent involvement can affect the behavior of parents enough to influence achievement. One recent summary of thirty-six studies of parent involvement concludes, "The form of parent involvement does not seem to be critical, so long as it is reasonably well-planned, comprehensive, and long-lasting. Even programs that just involve parents as reinforcers of what is being taught at school are effective. One-shot public relations campaigns, on the other hand, seem to have little effect."[3] In this context "parent involvement" means parents helping out with their children's education in various ways, particularly with home activities that help their children learn. The effectiveness of parent involvement may result as much from its effect on the children's attitudes toward school as from the specific knowledge children gain from their parents.

In House Bill 72 the legislature recognized the importance of parent involvement in student discipline, by including specific requirements for parent involvement in school discipline management programs and school-community guidance centers. However, strong general incentives for districts to develop and improve their parent involvement programs are missing from the legislation.

What incentives could the state use to encourage parent involvement? As with school improvement, the state has three basic tools it can use: prescription, financial assistance, and technical assistance, including dissemination.

- Prescription: The state could require each district to develop and implement a plan to involve parents and could make the examination of this plan and its effectiveness a critical item on the accreditation visit. The state can also require districts to assess the effectiveness of their parent involvement programs. For example, the district might select indicators of parent involvement monitor them systematically over time.

- Financial Assistance: Just as the state now provides money to districts to be used for bilingual education and compensatory education, it could also provide money to districts earmarked specifically for parent involvement activities.

- Technical Assistance: TEA could establish a Division of Parent Involvement specifically for the purpose of assisting districts to improve their parent involvement activities. As with TEA's other activities, the agency is likely to have the greatest impact if personnel from the Educational Service Centers repeatedly and frequently hold parent involvement workshops in the districts.

- Dissemination: TEA could attempt to identify and publicly recognize effective parent involvement approaches developed in different parts of the state. The agency could disseminate information about effective programs developed in communities of different sizes, socioeconomic levels, and geographic areas.

CONCLUSION

The reforms contained in House Bill 246 and House Bill 72 are a bold step in preparing Texas schools to meet the challenges of the next few decades. However, much remains to be done if Texans are to create a school system that successfully promotes both educational quality and educational equity. Because many changes in society are making the work of schools more difficult, the citizens of Texas and the legislature must be willing to accept the fact that education is likely to be more expensive in the future than it has been in the past. At the same time, there are virtually "free" resources, such as parent participation, that have not been adequately tapped.

Our survey uncovered widespread satisfaction with the general direction of reform, combined with concern over specific areas where implementation of the law has been difficult. We found that the goal of providing educational opportunities to students in poor districts comparable to those available to students in wealthy districts is extremely difficult to attain. The difficulty of achieving equal educational opportunity is all the more reason why Texans should pay increased attention to this goal in the future.

Notes

[1]Interview with Ernest Chambers, Director, Education Service Centers, Texas Education Agency, Austin, Texas, June 25, 1985.

[2]Telephone interview with Lee Laws, Director, Compensatory Education Programs, Austin ISD, October 17, 1985; telephone interview with Joan Burnham, Grants Planning Coordinator, Austin ISD, March 19, 1985.

[3]Anne T. Henderson, <u>Parent Participation--Student Achievement: The Evidence Grows</u> (Columbia, Md: National Committee for Citizens in Education, 1981).